laughing at gravity

Barnard New Women Poets Series

Editors: Christopher Baswell, Celeste Schenck

1986   *Heredity*, Patricia Storace

laughing at gravity

conversations with isaac newton

Elizabeth Socolow

WITH AN INTRODUCTION BY MARIE PONSOT

BEACON PRESS   BOSTON

Beacon Press
25 Beacon Street
Boston, Massachusetts 02108

Beacon Press books
are published under the auspices of
the Unitarian Universalist Association of
Congregations.

95 94 93 92 91 90 89 88   8 7 6 5 4 3 2 1

Portions of this work have appeared in
*Ploughshares, Greenhouse Magazine, The Vassar
Quarterly, The U.S. 1 Worksheets, Nimrod Maga-
zine,* and *The Nantucket Review.*

Text design by Linda Koegel

Library of Congress Cataloging-in-Publication Data

Socolow, Elizabeth.
    Laughing at gravity.
    (Barnard new women poets series)
    1. Newton, Isaac, Sir, 1642–1727—
Poetry. I. Title. II. Series.
PS3569.0374L38   1988   811'.54   87-42846
ISBN 0-8070-6804-7
ISBN 0-8070-6805-5 (pbk.)

For my sister
&
for the marriages of the season—
may they thrive.

All these things being consider'd, it seems probable to me, that God in the Beginning form'd Matter in solid, massy, hard, impenetrable, moveable Particles, of such Sizes and Figures, and with such other Properties, and in such Proportion to Space, as most conduced to the End for which he form'd them; and that these primitive Particles being Solids, are incomparably harder than any porous Bodies compounded of them, even so very hard, as never to wear or break in pieces; no ordinary Power being able to divide what God himself made one in the first Creation.

While the Particles continue entire, they may compose Bodies of one and the same Nature and Texture in all Ages: But should they wear away, or break in pieces, the Nature of Things depending on them, would be changed. Water and Earth, composed of old worn Particles and Fragments of particles, would not be of the same Nature and Texture now, with Water and Earth composed of entire Particles in the Beginning.

And therefore, that Nature may be lasting, the Changes of corporeal Things are to be placed only in the various Separations and new Associations and Motions of these permanent Particles; compound Bodies being apt to break, not in the midst of solid Particles, but where those Particles are laid together, and only touch in a few Points.

—Isaac Newton, the *Opticks*, book 3, part 1

Islands

O for God's sake
they are connected
underneath

They look at each other
across the glittering sea
some keep a low profile

Some are cliffs
The bathers think
islands are separate like them.

—Muriel Rukeyser, *The Gates*, 1976

Contents

III. *Epithalamion*
(of Freedom, Marriage, and the Unified Field)

Preface

THE ART OF LOVE with which this work concerns itself and the science Isaac Newton practiced depend upon a deep belief in transformations. Newton changed the landscape of the heavens, changed the nature of our mathematical concepts, and, for years, practiced alchemy. Before him, there was no concept of the attraction between distant bodies. And before he had arrived at a calculus able to sum the mass of objects into a point, he could not, to his satisfaction, demonstrate what he had seen many years earlier.

The bootstrap operation in which the celestial observations called out the calculus, and the calculus, in turn, refined the theory about planetary motion, his sense of such invisible forces of attraction, his arriving at the mathematics and coming to prove there was such attraction—is a remarkable story of courtship in a solitary and cognitive domain. I know of no story quite like it and commend the biographies of Newton that tell it, especially *In the Presence of the Creator* by Gale E. Christianson and *Never at Rest* by Richard S. Westfall. In addition, Frank Manuel in *A Portrait of Isaac Newton* has given a fine study of the family drama that would have produced a Newton. Reading backward, that form of psychoanalytic causality is interesting and inventive, and this work is indebted to the insights there.

In particular, Newton's move away from standard thought and vision to new ways of conceptualizing applied to his religious faith as well. He despised fuzzy concepts, and to him, a three-personed God, as John Donne called the Trinity, was an impossible belief. For years, he wrote of the Old and New Testaments in an attempt to understand, anthropologically, what lay at the heart of sacrifice. His name may have been suggestive in this regard, and a deeper sense of having lost so much may also have impelled him. Newton was, in fact, a closet Unitarian, who kept his beliefs secret for fear of losing his position at Anglican Cambridge.

These poems and meditations take Hannah Newton, Isaac's mother, and the son, Isaac himself, as the Muse and impossible lover. I have stated most of the relevant details of his life in the course of the narrative, but anyone who has tried to give information in the middle of direct address knows that is a cumbersome process. Newton was born in 1642 on Christmas Eve, premature and posthumous to his father, also Isaac. His parents had been married a scant six months when the father died. His mother went back to the Ayscoughs, her parents, and the home of her childhood in Woolsthorpe, where, in addition to the maternal grandfather, James, and the grandmother, Margery, there was also a maternal uncle, James Ayscough, a character who figures here in a manner that may be as legendary as the fall of the apple. In any case, Newton spent his first three years with his widowed mother. At that point, a man in his early sixties, the Reverend Smith, came courting. For whatever reasons, Isaac's mother agreed to a match that would take her away from the Woolsthorpe household and leave young Isaac with her family.

He was mechanical, and played with things, relating from the earliest age to objects and the world of objects he could control. He built windmills, studied sundials, and liked to make doll furniture which, it was said, he gave to the girls at school.

He was talented in school, though not immediately; when he was in his teens his mother asked him to keep her books. He hated accounting. But, since her brother, William Ayscough, had graduated from Cambridge in 1637, there was a precedent for going to university in the family that raised him. And this opportunity saved him from a life as a small farmer bound, weekly, to market.

In 1665 he was at Cambridge doing what we would call graduate work when the plague struck and shut the university down. He came back home and continued his work: scholars assign his discovery of gravity to that year; and between 1665 and 1666 he invented pieces of what would become the calculus. He also worked with the prism in his room, bending light and developing his theory of light and color. Until Newton, color was thought to inhere in bodies as an attribute of them. He understood that color was a property of light itself and went about proving that through his work with the green glass.

His next great work came almost twenty-two years later. In 1687 the *Principia* was published. This is the book that gives us the theory of attraction between bodies and the calculus from which it grew. Newton, who began by using the word gravity, stopped using it: distant bodies move toward each other according to fixed laws; it is not a simple, or not-so-simple, matter of one apple falling toward a stationary earth.

For more than thirty years Newton was the Lucasian Professor of Mathematics at Cambridge. In 1672 he presented his theory of colors at the Royal Society in London, and continued writing scientific articles published in *Philosophical Transactions*. His scientific investigations of matter and motion led to his appointment as the President of the Royal Society. He was appointed Warden and then Master of the Mint in his later years as a reward for his scientific achievements. In 1696 he left his post at Cambridge to carry on in London, where he lived until the end of his eighty-five years.

What I found compelling about Newton was his isolation, his terror of women, and his language first given to me as a freshman at Vassar College by a professor who thought introductory physics should not slight the fine seventeenth-century prose of the greatest scientist of that century. In 1958 she asked us to write a dialogue between ourselves, Newton, and Aristotle, and the form here owes her an enormous debt. That exercise let me see that, whatever his subject, much of his language concerns the pull between bodies, seen and unseen, and their disposition. He atomizes the world. Both the suffering and the play of words are evident to me in his attempt to mediate the intense pain he clearly felt in being alive and human. He fought bitterly with almost everyone of his acquaintance, Halley having been a prominent exception. He was never comfortable with people at close quarter. He never married or, to our knowledge, had anything at all to do with emotional or physical intimacy. He was a despotic leader, rigid in his practice, from what we can tell. He enjoyed dispensing property and money to relatives, supervised graduate students, had a friend in one Fatio de Duillier, a young Swiss mathematician, whom some people have wanted to take as a possible homosexual amour. Even if we allow him such a softening liaison, he is hardly sympathetic. In his fifties he fought with Locke, who he believed tried to embroil him with a woman, and at that time wrote a famous letter to the philosopher. My own reasons for choosing the prismatics of such an unresponsive partner for my musings emerge, I hope, from the text that follows.

Acknowledgments

I WANT TO THANK all the friends and family who have sustained me, and formally to acknowledge the support of the New Jersey State Council on the Arts, which granted me awards in poetry in 1982–83 and in 1986–87.

Members of the U.S. 1 Poets' Cooperative, the 92nd Street Y Poetry Center, the Princeton Research Forum, and the Robert Frost Place in Franconia, New Hampshire, have guided me with generosity for many years. Tom and Katherine Cole have nurtured me and the work. My gratitude goes to them, to Barnard College and the Women Poets Series, the Women's Discussion Group of Princeton, the Douglass College Institute for Research on Women, and to a few individuals who have helped, with particular focus, in creating this work: to Robert Woolfolk and James Binney for years of conversation on the subject, to Anne Goble and William Matthews who read successive drafts with a keen and generous spirit, to Carol Gilligan, Alicia and Jeremiah Ostriker, David Egger, William Gifford, Fred Chapell, Stuart Peterfreund, and Annette Allen, who responded to key pieces in their less-finished forms, to Martha Hannon who typed the final draft gladly in a short space of time, to Neil Hood, Linda Walko, and Ed Kozarski of the Princeton Quickprint Center who rescued me at many zero hours with fine reproduction, to Christopher Baswell, Celeste Schenck, and Marie Ponsot, whose optimism called the manuscript into publication, and, finally, to Joanne Wyckoff and Thomas Fischer of Beacon Press whose editorial assistance has been both cheerful and exemplary.

Introduction

MARIE PONSOT

HERE ARE Elizabeth Socolow's compelling poems. Though their demeanor is quiet, they are charged with feeling. Though their language, entirely poetic, is that of generative metaphor, its rhythms are often those of prose—a prose sometimes made eloquent with aphorisms, and the rest of the time made intimate in the voice of reflective inner monologue. Though Socolow uses the dominant convention of free verse, she also informs her work with a subtly linked music of assonance and interesting cadences.

They are active poems. The action is mental and eventful, full of vitality. It springs from concrete experience acutely understood. Socolow's poetic power is fed by a mix of cultural streams, rich enough that when she speaks her force naturally breaks new ground.

Habits of attention, observation, and questing speculation give her language urgency. I am reminded how intimate and exciting is the love of mind for mind, in the rarely identified, but everyday, grip of intellectual passion. Socolow can afford to entertain this passion because she puts it to essential use—nothing fancy. It's both effect and cause of the natural voice of the speaker of the poems, with its typical amplifying abundance and its bold connections.

At times, the poems reveal the speaker's life in flashes or lightning strokes, compressed by an almost desperate discretion. The effect is poignant, troubling. (Perhaps we're not used to this heroic readiness to tell the unheroic everyday truth. Here are libraries and jobs as well as diapers, electrons as well as breakfasts, and they are as much the occasion of loss or fear or joy as the more usual forms love takes.) In this way, from "the Big Dipper of memory where the sky walks like birds resting on the roof of barns," the truth of the speaker emerges. "In courage, I want to know the truth, don't you?"

These are poems of long breath. Many are built in long lines, with runs of unstressed syllables between stresses. Many are quite long poems. (For instance, the remarkable "To Newton: Of Freedom, the Plague, and the Unified Field" is composed in some 370 lines.) This gives Socolow room to produce excitement that's not itch-and-scratch but pervasive and satisfying. And in the big poem-as-a-whole, her cadences, turns, and resolutions have the space to show the rightness of their structure.

Memorable lines and sentences are easy to find: "that four-fold budpump of survival, our chromosomes"; birth, "that handclasp down the whole of us"; "Anger, in the end, is easier than loss, loss vague as the missing sound of a step that has been carpeted"; "We cannot be colonial in love"; "Marriage was an ark and not a marathon"; "We are in the recovery room all our lives." How different they are; what a pleasure it is to hear this original voice.

It's a further pleasure that the number of fine moments, places, centers seems to increase with each rereading. That is no accident; it's because nothing is simply noticeable on its own. What seem at first to be specially successful parts are more importantly generative of the larger whole to which everything's necessary and serves the cumulative value of connectedness. I think of "To Newton: Reading His *Opticks* Again." It keeps opening out into instances of many kinds and phases of love and need; by their amplitude and the way they complete each other, its twelve parts "breathe generosity." Here is the eleventh part:

> Put out the light and then put out the light.
> My older son, ecologist, has given me a candle-
> snuffer for my birthday. Brass butterfly
>
> resting open-winged on the inverted cup,
> the heft of this curved handle in my palm
> moves to douse the flame, two flames,
>
> as if the wrought butterfly would
> take off after a brief moment
> of such heat and rest and not return
>
> though contained in this meadow
> of some known breadth and depth.
> As scientists catch tagged
>
> *Oenius chryxus* in the mountains
> of Colorado and let them go,
> never thinking of Aeneas or of Christ,
>
> trying to find out how far they fly,
> how often meet and mate and what
> they feed on, we promise not to impede

the pattern of each other's lives
more than the instant it takes
this brass instrument to kiss

the moving flame. Like this
I want to say I love you; in such
fixity of hope and purpose,

such liberty of moving in these
ancient fields, their windows
of receding absence dance.

I move to where you are as dustmotes
travel on the slanting beam.
Newton, you are with me, gone.

The last tercet displays one of the ways Socolow calls on her vision of
Sir Isaac Newton—man of light and gravity—as metaphor. She is di-
rect. Time is entered, rather than transcended, to become the times
we live in. We end up in mind-time, the ultimate museum without
walls, where any object or subject may be found precious. "What's a
mere three hundred years to lovers?"

The great physicist is one of the chief persons-as-metaphor in this
well-populated work. Socolow also evokes Joe DiMaggio's son, Queen
Elizabeth I, Pierre Bonnard and the wife he painted, John Milton, TV
movie heroes, Teilhard de Chardin, Blake's and Princeton's tigers,
Blake himself, Saint Augustine, Eve seen through the eyes of her
daughter, Saint Francis, Lucy of Olduvai, the painter Juan de Flandes,
Newton's translator Emilie du Châtelet and her lover Voltaire, and fig-
ures from the poet's own family. Some of these are the speakers of the
poems in which they appear.

Socolow's way of summoning the presence of these people is more
than just restorative. With all of them she works changes quite differ-
ent from, say, Ezra Pound's salvaging of glorious images against our
ruin: changes which, by relating then and now concretely—not refer-
entially—remind us of the undying past we contain. We're in the
presence of the giants whose shoulders we stand on, giants in no
need of rescue, their ideas alive in us whether or not we are able to
name them. There are giants, in the human history our minds de-
pend on, and here in these poems they are at home to consciousness.

For Socolow, Newton is prismatic. He is her Muse, her beloved, her companion, a model for one mode of her thinking, the theme of her meditative scrutiny, the Virgil who leads her to scrutinize everything; he is Genius, a solitary, a sensitive scientific observer of relations and predictions and consequences, an intellectual in love with the mind's work in correspondence with the things of this world. As Socolow transfigures him, he is the central and extending metaphoric sum of all these. He is always, though long dead, vital, omnipresent, in the cosmic views and the methods of observation understood, which we owe him.

Though as ignorant of physics and mathematics as of Newton, I found myself at ease as I read. I was borne back or forward to how it must have been for most of human history, allowed to speculate freely, without the barriers at the limits of specialization which most of the time I too faithfully respect.

In the haunting light and gravity of the poems, the fake split of mental life into sciences and humanities vanishes; each appears ramified in the other, their many special features well rooted in ordinary consciousness. In turn, the ordinary consciousness like mine thrives, enlarged by Socolow's time-defying reach.

Newton's work and life are recalled—as in all memory—as synchronous in the mind, and so we meet him: as infant born to a father dead for months, as three-year-old boy sent away from (and by) his mother when she married for a second time, as grown man whose solitary existence is vividly inhabited by the abundance of a passionate mental life, as a mind many of whose conclusions are our ordinary, unexamined premises.

Even the difficult turn Socolow negotiates to show her personal love of the man Newton comes true, through a kind of delectation, through the careful attention she gives to reconstructing the events of his life, "trying, as women do, to understand their lovers." All facets of the prism are polished to refract light.

In similar ways, the rest of the people of Socolow's world are brought forth. The light of the turning prism catches Hannah, Newton's mother, at an oblique angle, among her quandaries. Consideration of images for this one woman, "mother like me," calls up others—the speaker herself, Eve's nameless daughter, Sarah and her son Isaac, Mary mother of Jesus of Nazareth, in a series of supple transformations, through which Socolow's personal and historical imagination shines. Such transformation is, I think, the single most important structural principle of her poems. Event, idea, metaphor, discovery are kept developing, developing, and never digressively. It may look at first as if she begins the change with a sort of kaleidoscope turn—one same set of elements, newly configured. But the configuration is neither fleeting nor static. It quickly takes on the virtual life Susanne K. Langer says we recognize in any art, as bits and pieces fuse and reticulate, and the poem is moving in a new way. Such *passages* (as André Lhote calls the dynamics of this kind of composition) are impossible to quote. But that's no loss, since the pleasure of the poems themselves is here before you.

I

evidence
(of him)

Emilie du Châtelet, Nine Months Pregnant, Addresses Newton: Notes Found accompanying Her Translation of Mathematical Principles of Natural Philosophy

Gabrielle-Emilie Le Tonnelier de Breteuil, marquise du Châtelet, learned aristocrat of eighteenth-century France, companion and colleague of Voltaire at the estate of her husband at Cirey, scientist, classicist, first translator of Newton's work into French, died in 1749 at the age of forty-four after giving birth to a daughter. In the twelfth year of their long association, Voltaire abandoned her sexually; she took as a lover Jean-François de Saint-Lambert, a young and not considerable poet who neglected her during her difficult, late pregnancy. She was depressed at his neglect as Voltaire was outraged at Saint-Lambert's ineffectual sexual technique. But Voltaire's outrage did nothing to alleviate the situation: just when Emilie needed support, entering middle age and the climacteric, Voltaire had fallen in love with a young cousin, a fact which Emilie did not, fortunately, divine. Desperate, pregnant, she duped her husband, who spent most of the time away from Cirey as a regimental commander, into a weekend of amour, all the household aware that she was already with child. The marquis du Châtelet either went along with the ruse, enjoying her full bosom of early pregnancy which she exposed maximally at table to seduce him, or was simply overcome with the old call of a tolerant and affectionate partnership. In any case all three men wept, Voltaire most inconsolably, at her death. Her infant daughter died either just before or just after her mother.

I think the roof of his house must be thatched,
one floor, no stairs, a parlor, kitchen, fireplace,
a slow incline to reach the entrance round a bend,
more a cottage, less a house,
in fall, a patch of aching yellow flowers at the steps,
and laundry hung out in the sun
at the ordinary, lived-in house next door.
That day you first thought these thoughts,
I suspect a golden robe on the line flapped

3

and flagged the late marguerites or marigolds,
I'm not sure which. Do colors echo? We say:
the washed robe matched the flowers,
and leave it at that.
My Lord, my kidneys ache. I shall not live, I know it.
Though there is ample history of ailing kidneys among us
Gallic writers. Montaigne, I follow you,
though the stone I must pass is a late child.
Newton, you are saving me with your finest distraction.
Your advice to men wracked by the urgency of desire—
not to ban visions of naked women but to supplant them with
thinking of particles moving in a black, meadowless space—
is my rule, though I could not be more unmanned than this,
at this late date. I ache. I write.

Such a long way back, I've watched to find how you scanned
the lacework of the stars that may have matched
the veined plaster walls you took to writing on.
Did your mother scold you
for marking the solid, white surface near your bed,
paper costly? Did she visit?
I want to enter the lonely mind that saw all things falling,
saw them bending toward each other in the night.

How desperate you must have been to stave collision off,
and keep, as precious, courtly stallions, or unicorns
in a delicate pen, the gossamer suspension
of that spider web you saw in motion round the sun.

My baby is penned in like that.
The globe of me wants to burst,
and I stay whole as the planets in their roundness.
In small rooms with white walls,
longing for the God I have dismissed,
as in a convent outside Cirey once,
or here, where I write, the walls' old plaster suggestively
cracked, I think I know the spinning English of your planets,
know your spirit hemmed in by the fixed construction
you had theorized, know your spirit in your solitary room
aware you had forgotten just out the window
the dazzling shine of winter stars.

4

To Newton: Of Small Changes

i
Small changes can be monumental.

For some it begins so simply
with ordinary life, a child born,
clamoring in the night for food.
We are man and woman, father, mother,
not alike, some ways, those that are
for beauty and smooth passage, wonderful.

How the other parent can awaken, bring the baby
safely to the sleeping continent the nursing mother
has become for this short span, can bring
the faintly talced baby in the soft, clean, cotton
nightgown, green stars on a white ground,
changed and sweet-smelling, to the big bed.

How even in her sleep, unable to lift her body
to stand up, the mother's hands gentle
the thin-shelled head and guide the howling place
to suck and answer, to become a mouth again
while the eyes search to know the geography
of the dark light in her arms, her eyes.

She finds the doors of garments, fills them
with the pliant arms and fingers, moves
the child's shapes, its warm flesh tenderly
as tongues of love, playing with sounds,
playing with the flexion of the knees and elbows,
their fine awkwardness. Some fathers who can rise
at any time of night know they are envious, wish

to give suck, give milk like the thin, blue wish
for fountains that quench thirst, fountains
that feel like you are swallowing even as they burst.

ii
Small changes can be monumental.

From that first saturation and delay,
from that agony of ease, handclasp down
the whole of us, that massive, first,
nuclear unfolding, we are
in the recovery room all our lives.

Of Newton and the Apple

Newton, having lost a father and a mother, twice,
found gravity and, I suspect, Love,
when he saw the apple,
or whatever fell that final time
to make him see how all things act like that,
he must have been amused
and even laughed out loud, alone,
and turned to tell the news
and knew, again, how unaccompanied he was.

I see the way he thirsted all his life
to find the force that seemed not to be there,
but acted, and precisely.
His natural father dead before his birth,
how he must have needed to compare
the moment of discovery to something
familiar, unexpected, like a father
who appears in a red cloak from above at dusk,
or like the sundial he found half-hidden in the cow parsley
of his mother's Woolsthorpe garden.

Maybe he made up the apple.
Maybe not. It was a kind of metaphor,
and, given peaches, how they flop to the ground
so readily when ripe, believable.
Apples hold on, dignified, hold together when they drop.
Joyous then, when he got it,
the idea, the way to tell the story.
And laughing out loud, though alone.
Would psychiatrists faced with such a man
deem laughter at gravity
inappropriate behavior?
He was hardly ordinary, after all,
intimate with celestial bodies only.

Those solar harvests sown like rhyme,
how they bring the future in the scattering.
The seeds of matter, falling, grow into a pattern
like words in a sestina.
How he looked to the heavens

for the plants and planets
coming home, glowing bright,
how things flow toward one another
against the obstacle of themselves
with little need of names.
The first apple didn't fall. We did.
Or so the story goes. It didn't fall. We took it.
And so, Love, maybe the second apple did fall,
like the second shoe.
Let's mix the gardens and the sacrifice,
see chrysanthemums in stars,
Orion's sword in Abraham's hand.
Let's call that first apple the accomplished
sacrifice, not averted,
shall we, while we're at it,
and knowing how much we lost
in the tasting?

To Hannah Newton: On Her Choice and Need

Hannah, how did you do it? Keep him alive,
then leave him? When the Reverend Smith
proposed, was the pull as much from below
as above? I hope so. And hope, too, it was
more than economic. The record shows
you asked your brother, James Ayscough,
about the wisdom of the marriage. How did that go?
The household thrown askew, did he ask you
if he could keep the child with him,
clear from the start your new husband
would not have an Isaac, or having one, needed
to perform a sacrifice on your behalf?
Three is so young to leave a child you had kept so close,
keeping him alive after such a birth.

Was the second breach abrupt, or did you find a way
to shape a second weaning? If there were going back,
if changing tables were the place of transformation,
if we could put our troubled lovers there, and
touch them everywhere with smiles and gentle
unguents, talcs and songs, if we could tender them
our love in touch and glance, and wish them whole
and sexual and well, could this heal? There is science,
and there is touch and tears and laughter.

I always knew they did that, parents,
laid together, touching only in a few points,
conjugal as compounds creating something new,
past all the curtains,
past all the obscurity,
and hypocrisy about what was really true.
I knew from the sharp fragrance
of my parents' room.

I could imagine the heaving, the crying out,
from my mother's long manatee sleep afterwards.
How she lay curled in her bed breathing deeply, my father
long out of the house on Sunday morning.
I could not wake her. She was that exhausted.
And I could tell the work of it—she could have been lazy

after a week of work like hers, but traveled
a little of the way to the labor of birth.
Ordinary people have such fine ways of making life go on.

Mother of his, mother like me, how can we save
this or any nation without nature, if
all we are to hold most high believes that touch
and sex are sin, and holiness akin to sublimation?

I went to the National Gallery and I saw
a Flemish Annunciation by Juan de Flandes
who went, at the cusp of the sixteenth century,
to Spain from the Lowlands, where he painted
holiness. In this Annunciation

the Virgin has her finger in the crease
of an illuminated book, her gaze
so lifted there's a white crescent
cradling the iris of each eye.

This is apparently the look of ecstasy,
the heavy book pressed on her womb and cleft,
text giving way to flesh. The angel comes here
from behind, sneaky as pleasure stolen

in a quiet moment, quiet room. His hand
is raised, with staff, as if to strike the girl,
virgin, but not chaste exactly.
The Angel's face is gentle as a younger sister.

He could be scolding her with words
for her disgrace: *If I catch you skipping*
to the good parts like this again
I'll slap you. The woman can't stop now,
caught at the very instant of cascade, collapse.

Breath evened, blush thinned, she smiles a little,
stands, accused, and tells the visitor:
You are my manufacture, sir. You come
from where I've gone, fetched from where
you prefer I go—with God you say
and mean alone.

Emilie du Châtelet, Thinking of Her Lover, Addresses Newton: On Isaac, the Old Testament, Sacrifice, and Marriage

Why won't you answer back?
I want to have your child—
our child I mean, share it, marry with you.
And you don't even answer when I write,
take months, years, wear me down, until
I must go back to what you wrote centuries ago
for solace. My beloved is mine, yes, I am his light,
he my refracting prism. I am bent colorful for love.
Winter nights I eat marrow,
my tongue indecent, searching it out.
We are all murderers, as you know.
Many ways to deal with that.

It is spring, and I have read your rabbi's writings.
That's what you were, half anthropologist,
half rabbi. How you tried calling the Hebrews *they*
to understand us all, and sacrifice, the forms
of slaughter that displayed blood on the communal altar.

Isaac, Christ manqué, the sacrifice averted,
the son given by the father, almost, the driven impulse
to do this: you knew what that act says
about the father's fear of losing power to the son.
Sarah is not mentioned in those verses of Genesis
in which the Patriarch takes their son to slaughter.

They never had a daughter
and the threat of losing that late son killed her, Isaac.
We have to read causality from position,
as with planets, so with text, as with motion, feeling.
And you, born on Christ's birthday, called Isaac, born
early and in great distress, not expected to live:
there is a theory out this year that would have us know
parturition nearly fatal makes all later parting
seem like death.

She called you a quart bottle, it went that hard
with you, come early, Christmas Eve, your father gone,
the necks of babies alarming anyway, for the way they seem

to neglect the head. She saw yours wobble like some planet
losing hold, sent her friends in cold December for medicine
against your death. *Isaac* she must have keened, *Isaac*
against the loss of both of you, practical and weeping, saving
you with milk and luck and medicine, one name cried
for two of you, struggling against the double loss,
she nursed and won.
The laws of life are these: when she left, after such
a birth and you only three, death or some discovery
of enormous magnitude was a necessity.
To prove there is contiguity across vast space
became the burden of your vision
once she had gone three miles to that new place
her second husband, very reverend, forbid you to set foot in,
she scarce, you miscreant, no doubt, in love.

To Hannah Newton: Of the Garden

Alone like that, with your brother
and the parents of your childhood.
Alone with a difficult boy, no embrace, and young
and needing change, I see what you did.
But to have to trade a husband for a son
a second time, having had a son supplant a husband
once: impossible request.
Imagine, for a moment, you had had a daughter.
Would you have kept her alive? What then,
when she was three? Would she have been so inconsequential
the Reverend would have had her?
And is that a blessing,
the slide to easy acceptance
for the total lack of threat we represent?
And what if there had been, as children
often say there must have been, daughters
of Eve, what then?
How would they have spoken in that garden?
Some days I think we can bear, now,
to listen to the daughter of Eve
in everlasting tribute to her patience.
See her, strong-armed with a light touch, one dark braid
down her back, like a sculpture by Matisse.
Made of rock, expectant, even urgent
in her patience. Her eyes are full of light.
She may just have been crying, remembering her mother.

The daughter of Eve speaks of the presence of God:

You should have seen the tree,
a poor-looking thing, gnarled and knotted,
older than you would have thought possible
in so much green.

Knowledge, you call it?
More like pity.
Her story was that she was sorry,

sorry for its neglect,
she told us, and ours in his thought, his plans.

13

Our mother reached, it is true, for the fruit.
As if wood and bark and sap

need to feel useful, like us.
There was only her thought, winding
like her hair, no serpent. She said
it is important to name the daughters
as well as the sons,
and leave them equal portion
in one's own death and life, which everyone,
it seems, has forgotten it was all for,
the point Job himself reached
that was different from before he knew God.
All his agony. The waste of his family.
Forgive the lecture. And please forget the mechanics
of time. Of course I know Job.
Our mother before him. She was only trying
to keep things Even, after her way,
trying to keep the pleasure alive,
the comfort of companionable mates

moving from that one place, the dark
in the vase where you can feel
the readiness for wine and seed,
gathering in the space like the next question
forming, the not-knowing

begging answer
from the gap
left among the bones when she was made.

O Hannah Newton, I am afraid of being vulgar
in your presence. Every question is an opening.
The gaps your son saw between hard bodies that God
meant not to be divided
exist in speech as well.
Fill them in, as grass
on a London street in summer relieves the cracks
in cobbles or in barren, gray concrete.
We will never know everything. And every filter
makes a different flower, stalk, and seed, and heat.
At last I can stay still long enough and trace your grown

son's play with light, with levity and meandering
forward and back like an eel on my father's line,
worm-baited and the silence of fishers on the bay.
In the shuttered light tears form, I see rainbows,
and laugh through the sadness, see you longing,
as I longed for my lost hope.

I dreamed I planted flowers in your garden,
marigolds and something blue, forget-me-nots, no doubt,
and this was amazing, shocking, because I was so stiff
from tussling with the borders of my own backyard,
jumping on the edger as if it were a pogo-stick to push
the ivy near the privet and keep the grass distinct from
shrub. Every muscle ached—my accounts neglected
for the urgency of flesh and ground—to sleep. I needed
to be turned, massaged, unwound like the earth
I left reluctantly at dusk.

And in that anxious state of neglected bills, I dreamed
I invaded the privacy of your son's garden,
as if I had not had enough.
I turned his earth, and smoothed his beds,
made furrows to hold seed. These days as I grow old,
increasingly the censor steps from behind the curtain of
the dream just before I wake. And asks,
impatient with my taste, if I cannot manage to avoid
these innuendos.

It is spring, and I have read his sacred writings, a Christian rabbi's
    texts.
As we find luck from catastrophe if we are to live,
from crisis, he found law.
I think he saw how the ancients
transferred their being to the thing they sacrificed,
the goat Azazel sent with their impurity to exile,
the sacred goat, given at the same moment to God.
Ishmael and Isaac. The double wilderness.

Every spring I go again to meet the earth,
turn it, give it seed.
I could be a man with his wife,
the way I need to tend this landscape,

crop and stroke and probe.
I could be a woman giving birth again,
the way I push at obstacles
and struggle with deep roots. Bills mount.
Work goes undone. I will not keep away
from the dark beds, cannot separate myself
from the need to keep them alive.
Half the plants die and half the time
the ground bears surprises I have no names for,
ferns and flowers and herbs. Hannah, they say
it was like this for your son. He could not pull away
from work, went without food, left candles
burning, lost manuscripts to the fires of neglect.
I know he tended your mother's garden,
dug the spade into the soil,
studied the fin of the sundial, how it reached
to be contained. He avoided the local children.
Grown, advised men struggling with lustful images
of women to concentrate on thoughts of particles,
and computation. There are labels for his sort, today.
At least he did not damage an unsuspecting bride
who married him for love and wonder
and found him horrified at coming close.

I am in your garden again, planting it, bulldozing the earth
so our wedding can take place there, your son's and mine
with antiphons and tropes. Somewhere along the way
Isaac has come to want this. I have asked him so many
questions spinning away from his name.
What if the ark of Noah were a vision of our matching,
a description before the microscope
of the chromosomal dance? Darwin and his antagonists
cavort together in this vision.

The Bible holds the crystal and the Christ
together in the alphabet and ark and flood
half our chromosomes
sloughed off to the amniotic sea, dead
as if they did not matter. And what if seeing that,
we can find merciful ways to play it out in sport and laughter?
O Hannah Newton, Isaac means laughter.
The people of the book might save us
if we dare to look.

16

To Isaac: Of Hannah and Sarah, the Mothers

In highest moments we so often weep, Love,
do we not, the sorrow is so bound to ecstasy?
And wars are born in times of plenty as often as from
famine, as children come from lack and keen abundance.

I think of your mother again.

Did she call you Isaac, your dead
father's name? Even as she changed your diaper,
smiling at your fat-cheeked faces, top and bottom,
smiling in the cold winter dawn, furious
at your howling in the dark, the candle sputtering,
the waking up, alone to you, your body
small and floppy as an old man's abandoned boot?

Did she call you Isaac, cleaning you, laughing
as she said your name? Or was it then she called
you Icky, Icky, shaking her head in amusement.
Did she invent a babyname even as, angry, and loving and
praying for your survival, she made you smooth and
pink again as the snowy sky, the small clouds of your sex.

I know how I smiled at the tarred buttocks of my sons,
saying in that gesture, anything they gave out afterwards
would be received somehow. She gave you herself,
the smooth, softworn nightgown, the warm milk, eyes
pondering your even-then intelligence, as you stared up at
her searching gaze.

Over and over we grow ready and overwhelmed.
We give up some spare portion of what once inhered.
Milk comes and comes. Or else it doesn't.
And what else can Abraham have meant, and Sarah, silent
always, and especially when she let the father take their son
to give him once as she once had given him to air and light,
pushed him into struggle and suck and sleep? She cannot have
been laughing then, when she let the father give the son
to Yaweh.
   "Abraham, don't do it. It's only that your loins last
night were hungry lions, angry, roaring, a small printer's
small mistake. This morning, you're empty, clean, and

want to move. You generalize as easily as I grow wet
when someone cries for help. Here he is, a grown boy,
and I pucker as if these figs could give out milk to shield
him from your intention.

"Because I gave him up—from womb, from breast—must you?
Top me? Give him up entirely? Is it jealousy
that sends you to the harshness of those deep rocks,
yellow as bruises, as the other one you sent from you,
Ishmael, to wander? Must you lay waste creation
in your urge for justice?

"This is a child, ours.
And not ours to give away at will. Let him choose."

I would hazard my best brooch, your mother naming you
Isaac thought of Sarah and all the silent women in such words.
All women have, for centuries. As if to ask in doubled silence,
squared and cubed: "What did my form and shape of creature
have to say?" Her name was Hannah, after all, a Matriarch.

And given hymns and heartbeats, the spousal spondee asking,
answering in the marriage bed and from that fourfold
budpump of survival, our chromosomes, and from
the placeless archive we call our heart, she must have heard
in the neat name, the square you came to love so well:
Aye zak, New'ton. I' sack New'ton: such a lubdub sounding
as the doctors with their stethoscopes attend, the beat and font
we carry in the prayerful fingers of our ribs.

And given hymns and heartbeats, the spousal spondee asking,
answering in the marriage bed and from that fourfold
names for children before birth with more finiteness.
We all would like both sons and daughters if we want children,
if we could have the landscape equally kind and friendly to
both sorts, if the world in its press for accomplishment
did not make it so hard to be careful and go slow.
Given how many things a parent must fit into a day,
it takes us longer to do everything.
And we reward quick production in this culture.
Caretakers earn little and struggle all their lives,
or leave off caring to earn more success.

18

But champagne and cognac turn in attentive hands
in the dark caves for years of waiting, years
of growing body,
spirit,
effervescence. In people, we like our stars young
and long-burning,
cool, and distant, free of kids.
Rushing stars make fearsome parents.

We can be certain, Newton, your mother knew she had to have
a living child, your father dead, even as his gift was
quickening.

Carrying on alone:
half of us have had to do that because the press up
ambition's ladder claims our mates. Carrying on alone:
was it then—imagine it was you, Isaac, put yourself
in her place—was it then, when your husband died,
you named your consolation, Isaac, hearing the assonance
with Christ,
your son born on Christmas Day, between one and two in the
morning?

I can see her wrestling with her God, saying she would
give up this unborn child to have her husband back.
And was he, like you after him, a reluctant lover,
a bachelor who married and died at thirty-seven, a groom
of a few months, shocked, perhaps by the laws of physical
bodies, his manhood defined by the recoil from the women
bound, then, to the nurseries, the return to a woman's touch
read as feebleness therefore?

I am unmanned, he cried, perhaps,
at the surprising transformations of his flesh,
how it will not stay still, get set, however rigid,
O, it will bend and spill and be another thing come
morning. "Come," beckoned Hannah to her husband
walking in the afternoon, a sick call paid,
a Sunday after church, falling leaves and all melancholy
sifting down, snappish gusts gouging large bites
from the trees, and more and more leaves left,
it seems, despite that desperate consumption

19

of the branches' lungs. But we know it wasn't autumn,
though I place it then. It must have been June or July,

and balmy weather, the seduction of air that is palpable
and insistent as the gentlest, skillful lips and hands.
Perhaps the constant touching, all those unseen kisses
of the wind altered his customary no, and he consented
and had to give his life for such surrender.

Was his the sacrifice contained in the name Isaac?
"Come this once," she said, and gladly, afterwards,
would have given the son for the father, and later did
though it was all the other way around
until she tried it. "Am I not more to you than seven sons
and seven jobs and seven daughters?" every father cries out
some lost night. "Yes and no, depends when, both needed,
all, none possible in joy without you. And I: am I not
more to you than seven trophies, seven battles won,
your opponents bested in the field and all the newer,
younger women dull saltless bread?" you might have answered
with a question, like any Matriarch and Christian of us
asking the body back. Brief wafers. Heavy wine.

The Matriarchs were sacrifices long before the Romans
took the virgin Jesus. Thinking of the absence of carnal union
in our lives, Hannah Newton, I remembered you

and thought of Isaac, his fastidiousness. How long I waited for
ordinary books growing up, seven years before I could read
myself and cross the street to the public library

with high windows, too much heat in winter,
the fine smell of waxed oak and metal stacks,
where, when I had my fill of sentimental animals and Indians

of nurses marrying doctors, I returned to *As You Like It*
and Demosthenes at adolescence and first read about your life.
I paused at the second marriage, happy for your mother

and the Reverend Smith, two daughters born, another son,
and you all of fourteen, voice changed, I thought,
although such articles did not then mention that.

20

I saw you had to undergo your second father's
death, read of your schools and shocks,
your windmill, waterclock, and sundials, and saw how

she must have thought she left you just enough
alone, and praised your work and gave you to her brother
to encourage. But she was in shadow in all accounts
of your great light, like some solar twin hinted at

by the scholarly form of life that grew, and never
clearly seen in thirteen million years, or something like.

II

circumstance
(of him and me and emilie du châtelet)

To Newton on Balconies

I. THE THEATER OF GRAVITY AND MARRIAGE

There were balconies in the marriages of my childhood,
not for playing the romance of Romeo and Juliet falling in love,
but for mothers with graying hair. Ice clinked small summons
in the late afternoon, the cocktail glass held high, names
of the household children called, and we, their guests, called
with them. From the balcony, to it, we ran,
and the inevitable honey-colored dog raced to the raised voice
just ahead. The smell of dog preceded that frantic swaying
of the gold hindquarters up the stairs. The smell of dog was
in the rugs we played on, turning cartwheels, dealing green,
pink, blue Monopoly bills for games that went on half a week
of afternoons.

There were balconies and pregnancies that overhung
the rooms we played in, the slightly puffed eyes of Sarah's
mother that made me wonder, even before anyone knew
the thrill of that one new baby in a house
born after we could have babies of our own, the doubled
mystery of knowing from the inside that power.
There were balconies where babies slept under white mosquito
netting, common then, before the dull, gray, sturdy, plastic
screening my own sons summered under. Balconies, and,
occasionally, the hushed mention of affairs, alcohol, depression,
other trouble vague as smoke. Death there surely was, early,
concrete, accidental, but no broken homes where I grew up,
not the deliberate contest we came to as the century climbed its
stairs.

We feared fights, battling parents, and had our best hiding places
from the terror of that under the piano, behind thick curtains.
Anger in the end is easier than loss, loss vague as a missing
sound of a step that has been carpeted. I got lost only in
museums. In the nearby Metropolitan, I climbed the great
central flight of steps to the Chinese urns at the top, their
orange birds, blue dragons, flowers, willows. Ming, Ching,
Sung. In those years I tried to memorize the phylogeny of
oriental art and only got the music of the English names.

Just there, beyond the porcelain, the balcony looked down on
the great entry hall and doors, or, to be exact, I looked down,
my hands resting on the wide stone rail.

The rotunda of information was so far below, I had to tell
myself it would seem closer when I got older, taller.

Newton, distance shrinks with time, according to the laws of
human growth. And in this human calculus, needing to talk
again with you, as with a proper husband, needing to forget
the disconnection of all these marriages, the tragedy I still deny
of affection travestied in my own, I went to see the Roman
statues once again and the visiting treasures of Byzantium.

On the way to that store of ancient wealth, I saw a mother
hold her toddler on the wide stone railing twenty feet, at least,
above the marble floor. The small child dressed in yellow
sat defying gravity, as if falling was impossible.
The mother told the child: "Look. Look. See all the people
coming in the doors." Love, you gone, or perhaps imagined,
never really here, the sick sensation of plummeting was faster,
steeper than in childhood for that moment, or in dreams. I
wondered why until I understood I was no longer saying
to myself *then, when you are grown, it will seem less far
to fall.* Then was now, and I was wandering tall and alone, all
thought of such protection gone.

II. BREAD AND CIRCUSES

The movie on TV shows an engaged couple
fighting for a marriage. "I can't help it,"
the young woman, beautiful enough, is saying.
"Anyone on the street. Any man. It's like
those dreams of falling, the way I'm pulled.
I feel so frightened first, and afterwards.

so wasted and unclean." Her fiancé is actor-handsome,
tall, lean, and unperturbed, his eyes
fixed kindly on her fear. "Do you still
want to marry me," she begs, "if you know
this truth?" She is mightily afraid of marriage,
we understand, afraid of promises that preempt

a future vague as dry wilderness. He comforts
her. He wants to hear her thoughts. She interests
him as much as whatever he is thinking. They
do not speak of schedules or family.
The do not mention nature, food, or God.

How can I tell you and not sound idiotic?
Once, alone in the house and more than once
to test that first surprise, I cooked *osso*
buco, soup bones heavy with pale marrow.
I sucked the bones to whistling as I stood
consuming what was once the source of flowing blood.

Felt afterwards like the TV woman. Except
I knew I wanted plates, napkins, lively conversation,
the full bones of life eaten slowly enough
in company to seem remarkable. I remembered
the delicacy of campsites, the pine and raspberry
shrub in the New Hampshire woods, the way

tomatoes boil in the can like geraniums in ecstasy
and transformation. They look about to fly from the broth,
before being eaten on crusty bread in the open air alone.
And I could half believe there might be such
restraint that springs from the sense of something

there alive, there too, disturbing and thus begging
mere acknowledgment. It would offend the trees
and rocks, the order of creation to watch me eat
unaware of what has died: bean, grain, yeast, meat.
Watching the TV show, my son observes of language:
"There is no negative in English for a man who

sleeps around the way she does. What's she disgusted
for? Men act like that and score. They win. They
know their women. Every which way, know. At least
in French there's a word for that emptiness in either
gender. Though little used of men." Such summary
of the action, delivered with an offhand smile,

is my nearest anchor in a world where people
fall from lives at five-year intervals.
My son is just sixteen and says: "It takes

more carefulness than conversation, sex.
Don't you think?" Newton, what comes next

is often hidden in the blind. Lost like that,
you were as defenseless as I, at least once
had to apologize for imagining your friends
put you together with a woman. The tiger moves
through the flaming hoops. The linked elephants
tell the jugglers everything is separate,

shapely, joined. Listen to the whispers of circuses:
passion disciplined need not burn, and repetition
is lively not boring. Practice makes entertainment
not perfecton. There is dung all over the sand.
In your absence fixed laws have lifted
to this randomness. Is there nothing but activity?

I have four more years before the children leave.
Please let me keep. Two of them to see through.
I talk like that alone at an evening meal. Do so
because that first year walking home from school,
stopping at the first print that made sense, I read, or thought I read

a circus tragedy I could not forget: an acrobatic
act to heighten drama had the net removed
in mid-performance, just before the most unnerving
tightrope feat. And as the fanfare burst the vaulted
space, and the woven ropes dropped to the littered
ground, a child, four years old in the top balcony,

leaned over the rail and plummeted to death.
And oh, I knew, standing on 86th Street in the rain,
reading the paper at the covered wooden shed
where the cripple sat protected under tiers
of gum and candy, it was not suicide and no intent
to fall. She was trying as hard as possible to hold on,
and saw, clearly, how the act could end. The press
of vision brought her to her feet. Impatience moved
her stomach to the bar, and she leaned, Newton, leaned
in a world gone wild, where dependency can seem like suicide.

Emilie du Châtelet on the Colors of the Sun

On ne sait point la raison de cette surabondance de
rayons jaunes dans la lumière de nostre soleil, peut estre
dans autres soleils, les autres couleurs dominent elles,
peut estre mesme y en a t'il qui sont composés de cou-
leurs dont nous n'avons nulle idée, car qui osera borner
la puissance de celuy qui les a tous faits? *

—*Emilie du Châtelet*, Essai sur les Opticks de Newton

That's what she thought, Emilie du Châtelet,
and worried about barbarian women killing their babies
in the night. She tried to conjure the desperation
behind such snuffing out, the sun gone out for them, become
some screaming color in a famine. Cooler she was
about science and the contradiction of a boundless God
who would choose a yellow sun, as if there were
monotony, no dawns she ever saw, for sleeping through them
all, no brilliant red and purple sunsets noted
from her study. For more than gold
she had to posit suns elsewhere,
and we might have told her even here
we see according to our apparatus: other creatures, we suppose,
see our very sun in true orange all day long,
or black and white, a lit bulb in a gray sky.
And why not galaxies with an extra sun,
while she's at it, two suns,
like eyes, like an artist attending a bird just flown away?
We look at the night sky, reaching back,
some say, to the brush of comfort as we stared
at stars in those eyes that held us and formed us
and did not murder us in the earliest nights of rocking,
first arms, first chair.

---

* "We don't know any reason for the yellow rays in the
sun, their superseding all other colors. And maybe in
other suns, other colors dominate. Maybe there are even
suns made of colors we have no idea of, for who would
dare to bound the power of the one who made them all?"

Laughing at Gravity

I am ready to laugh at gravity, so many
true stories I do not know how to tell.

This one was funny, even as it happened,
though it felt portentous as Milton later
felt when I read his sentences about
the loss of everything fall on and on in
swelling cadences I saw him make
by wearing heavier boots each month
and pacing as he wrote. And it was beautiful
as his wordy garden or those I knew
of substantial tending and fragrance
in later Italy and England, wild and pruned,
the troubling tumble of flowers and careful
arrangements.

This thing I saw, or knew, was funny, beautiful,
and portentous, and I was four, which makes it
unbelievable as well, because I never forgot
and I am weightier now with so many years.
This was the image through which I knew
everything else of its kind, how I understood
all the people who never heard the word
cosmology to use for themselves, like Mary I
loved and knew that year, my sister's nurse,
who stopped talk like this by saying
now that's the truth. And sometimes they were
happier and knew more how to get that way
than I did, and sometimes they were trying
without the word to make sense of their worlds,
trying just as hard as anyone, against a thinness
and weariness of too much work and too little
surprise, hoping it all wouldn't always be
the way it was.

My mother did not trust my baby sister would
be wanted, and smothered her in attention and dismay.
I went to the beach and taught myself
to hurl myself in surf and feel the grinding stones,
to know the hurt I felt for her who came after me.

One day, swum out and exhausted, body flung
to stillness on a faded towel, pink or blue—
such lapses make me know how much the later vision
crowded memory of the ordinary things—
fingering the tufted nub of terrycloth
and the abrading sand in turns,
wanting to escape and not to die,
knowing by sand and towel
the grainy quality of nature,
the building up of dots,
thinking about the sandpipers' footprints
I had not counted but seen as connected
wishbones, watching, how, exactly,
the sandpipers moved, how quickly
they seemed to spill along the shore
like the dots on an antic typewriter
if I did not pick my finger up,
all the many hops making a flat waterfall
of dark bird with gold specks—

seeing all that, again, somewhere,
not in the sand, but in my—I had to say—
mind, pressing on my stomach with all my weight
on the terry and sand bits doubled in graininess
to feel the place inside where I would
carry a baby and love it as my sister
was not loved, no matter how it looked,
believing it would one day be able to be loved
and work in the world, which is what
my mother doubted in my sister who was
a girl, so doomed by infant chunkiness
as if it would not change a thousand times,
I had enough.

I turned on my back on the beach
and think I glimpsed the water's edge
and on the wet sand licked by tide
my own enormous footprints near the frail
birds' whose trail I could not read
any more than the letters set in linoleum
in my room, though the shapes looked like
writing, and though I was trying, at home,
and knew ABC. And saw,

but not there in the sand, and not solid,
not real, not out there as in a dream, but
in my mind what I had not seen before:
how big my footprints were, how small the birds',
how carefully I always sidestepped not to crush
the tracks and leave to the waves all those indentations
to take, in that way, the writing.

I watched the tide pull the darker shadowed places
into ordinary sand.
It was all right for waves to erase
but not for me to crush—
though I watched the daycamp children play a game
stepping on birdtracks before the waves
and that seemed fine for *them.* For all I know,
that's what makes a writing soul: a reticence
to wipe out the marks before they have been read.

My pulling back from what those children did
was no way absolute. It was even fine to think
about overprinting the birds' thin sticks with
the kidney-foot of me, satisfying if I had known
the birdfoot well enough that it would touch me
indelibly there where I stood up on this huge
edge of land at such an early age and did not fall.
I saw kidney-shapes in feet at four
and was amazed.

I took my father's journals,
the pictures of purpled cells,
bits of cabbage floating in red lakes,
growing flowers of flesh and sores like spilled gas
at Benjy's Sunoco on a rainy day,
and diagrams of hearts and lungs
and photographs of pregnant women.

All the people had black erasers
across their eyes, as if that way
they had no names. I saw footprints
looked like kidneys in the sand.
My father showed me that one shape
and said the name, his special work,

and unrolled the long gray strips
of heartbeats like the pipers' footprints
in the sand. I turned

on the faded towel from my stomach to my back.
And first there was a flock of birds that danced
like a sweater pulling to twisty thread
without knots, without cord, just the motion,
my mother knitting or unknitting a cable stitch
after a mistake, winding roses out of air.
The birds flew up and down together
for no reason, their play useless as the waves
wrinkling for no set purpose, fluted piecrust,
the bread dough pushed up like a river
flooding in the movie of the dam, like my mother
getting dressed in too tight clothes.

The most interesting things were always useless
as candy but more beautiful and alive, because,
like an accordion or cardiogram, what they were
and what they signified, changed, and moved, and breathed.

I got lost for the first time in those overhead birds.
And when I came back, I was crying at what I felt and saw,
the ordinary clouds, blue sky against which the birds
had played their hallelujahs as if I wasn't even there.

The clouds were the flatter kind,
like fish connected in a school,
like footprints, mine, enormous,
I could imagine, easily, the gigantic
airy bodies growing up from those white soles,
as my body grew up from my feet, as someone
might see me, if the beach were a plate of glass
and they alive in their sunken graves beneath,
or as the fish under the window on the floor
of Mrs. Stimpson's yacht I never rode but heard about
might see my feet from the ocean's heavy air.

The feet in the clouds I knew were only clouds,
walked on the thin shell that held them up
from earth, and they were pilgrims, slow at that border

as the sandpipers were fast at the edge of land
and water. And though I knew it was not true,
I laughed, and because it was not true and I had
thought of it and heard the joke, where?—
and saw, where?—the soles of pilgrims' feet
were souls risen,
I turned, and saw no one was there to tell,
and never likely would be to show how they
had all gone to heaven trouping like the campers
away from the hot sun.

Which, Love, is why I see you turn like me
to tell someone of the falling bodies
and find no one, particular and actual as that day and me myself,
and which, Love, is why if you
at four had been there, we both would have seen the clouds
and laughed about the scene
and which, you being where you are and unsuspecting
of this length and depth of need
is why I write this truth, best as I can.

To Newton: On Riding Horses
and the Gravity of the Fall

I don't remember where we kept the horses,
large things to lose, even in memory,
the backs of them quivering small promenades
of passion, like the air gusting a lake
to texture and brief darkness.

I see her ahead of me on her horse,
her straight blond hair swinging faster
and in rhythm with the horsetail's swish.
I see our two horses tied to trees
in that dim forest. They eat from oat bags.

Hard-pushed, we didn't ride them fast
but often enough up steep slopes, through
narrow places. Low branches bent us to
horse-shape, our bodies filling in the cradle
of their backs. We guided with the simplest reins—

bare legs against bare backs, manes
in our hands, sneakers pressed to withers,
no stirrups. The fine hairs on my legs caught
the August sun. More than riding the Atlantic surf,
the dips and swells of the Nantucket beach, more

than building blocks on the nursery floor,
I loved the solidity of horse bristling under me.
Stars scratched the sky like that, fine points
of light. I first learned the positions that summer,
stars in the sky so cold, when God cried, the tears

in the blackness turned to ice, tossed for us to steer by,
lost. Alice had the horses. Her father leaned
on the enormous medicine ball and showed us
how to worm-jump across the laces, body flat then standing,
balanced, and laughing in balance as the ball rolled

like an asteroid under our walking. Called,
he taught us the stars that one weekend I stayed overnight
with the other daycamp kids. More than the stars

and their moving, fixed positions, those two summers
of liberty across the bridge in New Jersey

given us to roam alone, back only for me to scurry
on the bus, back only then to the other eight-year-olds,
or whenever we wanted to swim with them, which must
have been almost every day, more even than the trust
of being chosen wise enough and canny-bodied

to accompany this child, unhurried daughter
of the camp directors, all of us silent in conspiracy,
never telling my parents we agreed to violate
the daycamp program they sent me to,
more than the mystery of acceptance or being here

with Joe DiMaggio's son, who got girls to eat
saltines on the bus and chew the wax paper wrappers
with him, making the wad last all the way to the City,
I loved Alice, the way her warm eyes vanquished all
risk and objection. I saw in her mother's casual wave,

as we rode off, the triumph of joy itself. In this Greek play
the Chorus says: *When a mother blesses a daughter,*
death and rivalry melt to fuel adventure. Only less
than this chance friend, the horses moved me,
their attentive answer to the burdens they wore

like barnacles, us, so attached at pleasure's platform
of release, the soft oysters of us singing
the imperfections of the sandy tracks. The eloquent
nostrils of horses still tell me smell is our first
knowledge of comfort, shame erased. This is

the Italian pastoral whose shepherd sings:
Passion's purpose is nothing less than ease and grace.
Those afternoons of horses healed me, plumbmark of later love,
its friendliness and attentive eyes, quiet,

and the grounded boundlessness. At seven, silent
mainly, we mentioned the next bend, next step, danger.
No one called us tomboys. We had long legs

and the exercised bodies of athletes. We felt so fine,
it never rained. In gloomy weather we curried

the horses, played in the main House, green turreted
as any castle, played Chutes and Ladders, talked
of animals. Rain fell of course, but where we curried
the horses I can't find, though I search the Big Dipper
of memory, where the sky walks like birds resting

on the roof of barns. Maybe it wasn't like this
every day, but only sometimes. It was enough. In sun
we moved to the horses' gaits and talked of how to hoof
the next logs single-file and not scare our dismounted,
naked carriers. We planned which trees to climb,

saw how bark bit star-formations in our thighs
and fingertips. Bearded moss scared us. We told dreams.
Dared each other to walk across skinnier logs, hang
in air over dry brooks. Half the time I collapsed
in shame to sit across a log-bridge, learned

how legs have a way of starting to shake and burn
just about halfway over to the other side.
Straddling narrow wood in shame made me want the wide,
warm saddledip of horse again, until it hurt
to have my legs apart, and I had to stretch them climbing.

One tree in particular it took us half an hour to find
the courage to go down. We had to scare ourselves with
the nightmare of falling through the thickened air,
the ground opening, the will of gravity to have us
plummet faster, free of fingerholds, free

of everything we wanted to hold on to. We
told each other how we violated trust, parents
missing us, and forced our muscles to grip and shinny
down the long, too bony trunk of that copper-skinned
tree. I had no name for luck like that, combined

with will. No near-death I've known has been more binding,
shared, or seen. We hugged each other at the bottom,

weeping for our lives, and laughing from a high
and wrinkled stone, climbed the horses. They had
small-noised us down the tree, worried through

whatever horses use to worry with.
We were too near the sky. Maybe that was what they saw.
And know that skidding on ice the night I almost
killed myself and the four women with me on the way
to our men, and we caught whirling at the edge—

a breath-slicing drop, sheer as the moments before shared sex,
I remembered that embrace at seven, full and brief and wise,
and the protective horses. It's my measure of what we all
want, even now, the holding in the moment of long terror,
the laughter in coming through. No work takes precedence,
no deadline preempts that scare into life

and all its winking emissaries. The yellow buses lined
up to take the campers home, waited for Judy to be sick
and Joe DiMaggio's son to pick which girl to chew
wax paper with. Sometimes his famous father was waiting
on the corner over the bridge. I half slept.

Alice, her parents, their pleasure in nature: it felt
like home I left, people who knew how to dredge a lake
from a declivity in sandy, Jersey soil I had to leave
every afternoon, and then, it seemed, forever. Newton, it hurt.
Like leaving the one best life. Imagine missing

Cambridge, having to go on with your mother's books, keeping
records of money, not stars. What would have happened
to you and us you changed the world for? Orion is clear
tonight. I love you for your fierce gentleness, the belt
a support, straight line meaning curve and return,

and not an instrument for punishing children. Newton, if you could
come back often enough to drink night with me, falling
toward each other, this gravity would lift. I am at liberty
in this attachment and often as lost as when I held
those first, most simple reins.

To a Friend of Newton:
On Gravity as the Source of Pleasure

i

Ball bearings he would have liked.
And, at a distance, to see how we would stand,
poised, each wearing one of a pair of roller skates,
promising each other we would pump together,
counting strides with our shorter, unwheeled leg,
promising we would hold hands until balance
and laughter demanded we let go.

We waited at the top of the hill,
breathing deep before experience
and gravity's way with us.
Because of this, the sound of roller skates
on concrete, the roughened wheels, sparks
flying seemed adventure's flint.
For romance the music of ball bearings
can't be touched by the lonesome call
of railroads, the whistle and empty tracks.

At six years old, unable to walk,
flattened by something like polio
you spent a year in bed, and healed.
The slight stiffness in your thighs,
when you were ten and we first met,
spoke a miracle to both of us, spoken of,
once in fourth grade in those first weeks
learning about mummies and papyrus
and Cleopatra. That year of stillness

was a shadow as we grew round, grew
breasts, and friendship found simple risk,
your real body flying thank-yous in
Leonia, New Jersey. Bound to the concrete,
we roared our moving legs over the best hill,
losing breath and contact, one of us
racing ahead for the sound of metal
and the speed we wanted.
That lost year of paralysis was
an angel in a high bed, discarded snakeskin

of your real body now
flying past clapboard houses—
then home to your mother's still-dreamed-of choice
and order, her Saturday refrigerator, the three ribbed
plastic holders packed: tuna salad, egg salad,
pink deviled ham. Your parents had the first mulch pile
I knew, the sexual smell of leaves
and late passion in the yard
and house, Scotch in the air, Spenser's
Britomart, psychology and smoke, piles of college papers
everywhere. We both had to be
professors because of them.

We both wanted to be like both of them, except for
the smoking. They taught me to lie white,
taught me to read feelings ahead of time
and spare them, if I could,
scolded me the one time I made curiosity
and truth query why
vice was so hard to lick, smoking to the point of
wheezing in the night what I meant.

Years later, reaching for hope, I joined them
in reaching for tobacco, and knew
the answer to the question I hurt your father with
and drew your mother's wrath from.
I wanted with you what was so easy anywhere
I had a calm home and a true friend: normalcy. Tears
and talk, good food, and exercise and laughter.
I drove every weekend to your house
that last year of an impossible childhood
and was amazed at the softness of your family's eyes,
your skin with the universal freckles
and shine of wet soap. I told you
the worst shames, the dread camping trip at fifteen to Nova
Scotia, bathing in the clear stream seeing my nakedness
among the high, pointed Norwegian spruce, that seemed
called down from the steep cliffs by gravity.
Newton was my rescuer
from that rape.

He jumped me from behind, the man, half a boy still,
that shocking, no warning in so much silence

in the woods where I'd gone from the campground
in Newfoundland, wild with jagged evergreens
biting the blue sky.

Fifteen, the only girl among all those boys,
I went to find a place to bathe,
and walked an hour,
and heard nothing, though he was behind me
all the while, that good at tracking. I had
undressed, and dipped into the cold, cold spring,
soaped myself in all that wilderness, and rinsed.
I was watching the way light
falls on water, seeing the solid stones, gray,
round boulders and my shoulders foreshortened
above them in reflection, my real legs wavy
underwater, so pink and almost as insubstantial
as the trees I seemed to walk among,

when he hit from behind, knocked me backward
into the bracing cold. The boulders dug into my real
and sensible back. My hair pulled out with the current.
And I thought of waves, light, the trees, the water
ruptured as I fell through it, his face in labor against me,
and, shocking, defying gravity, the branch of him

outstretched, the first penis I ever saw erect
pushing at my crotch. I hardly knew him.
I thought of my body reflected
in the water, the trees so far away, not falling in.
Look at yourself in the water. Look at your face,
I cried at him, clawing. He pulled away.

Newton saved me, what I knew of physics at that age
kept me more than what I knew of bodies.

ii
The color of graph paper moved you, finitude contained
in a grid of projected infinity made me feel alive.

iii
And all our sympathy went into our planning
for our parents, their old age, frightened at how they forbid
us to care for them, ever, even then, later on.

By then we were nineteen, had seen the couples at the old-
age camp where we were counsellors for the little kids.
We were twenty and engaged. You married, well, thank God,
one of us answered in all that human preparation we gave
each other, skating down those hills, panting up. We spoke
of things without, I think, a repeated conversation.
Only the walls and rooms, your brother's voice,
your father's tuneful laughter through his cough.
The ordinate of home ready in comforting silence to speak
to our abscissa of rising talk. We played word games, wrote
together, danced, plotted equations, endlessly, I remember.

iv
The color of graph paper moved you;
finitude contained in a grid of projected infinity
made me feel alive.
I have been reconsidering Newton's Law of Distances
in this light. The grainy picture
of even the most advanced TV
would have pleased him, I keep thinking,
a small allegory of the bodies of light traveling in air,
the sense of things absent become immediate.
Television means seeing far
they told us in fourth grade, when TV was
sometimes still called by its whole name
like a baby just brought home.
The graininess on the screen was
the sky and all its midnight stars compressed.
There was no color. And how the light traveled
to the room, how the images were brought, like good news
and the mystery of
ghosts in real space and air, palpable and turning:
this would have caught his attention
as it catches mine. Sometimes I confess, I cannot lose myself
in the story. I look at the *pointilliste* news
and want to know how the thing works.

The cat turns it on by sitting on the square
teats. In winter the odd light greets me
when I come home.

v

After a usual working day
we come to a cold house,
somewhere in each of our lives,
this moment, repeated, alone,
cold even with the lights turned on,
even with the familiar cracks and pictures
on the walls
and the reassurance of known dust
and angles of light.
It's home, but the nose is cold.
Probably you keep your coat on
even as you read the mail.
You listen to the furnace blow
after your finger's small beckoning.
It whines its old note of heat.
Alone in your teaching city,
your daughters eat supper 400 miles away,
at home with your husband for another working week,
and you at home with your calm knowledge of his love,
your certainty of the magnitude of your own for him,
and for the children. It is bigger than the sky, as children
say, bigger than the field the starlings feed in. I find
a feather near the catbox, no sign of the bird.
My sons are with their father and his wife. I hold
the feather, and the absent bird flies free, I am that glad
for you, for what you hold. All this you've made.

I hold it, and wonder about the old friends who shaped
coherence. From luck? And that first knowledge?
Again I want to ask you did you see the TV series
from the BBC where the most beloved father plays the cello
for respite from the overly familiar and routine, composes
rapt? In this show, the great actor
plays a character with daughters. He is compassionate,
in charge of a dozen poor old men, a choir leader
in the chapel, and when he has time

he turns to music, the long strings, the body
of curved wood between his knees. When pressed
in trying conversation with zealous fools
who style themselves his enemies, his eyes grow small.

His instrument not near, the actor's fingers reach
toward his chin and across his chest. His hands hold

a cello-shape of air. And he grows calm, breathing deep
as children poised to skate down the best hill in town,
even as his music, his mind, his hands pull, and I

reach for a hand, playfully attuned to what is or is not
there.

To Newton: Reading His Opticks Again

i
I enter this leather book and the words
become as comforting as beads warmed
in my hand. I can believe my eyes touch,
in their way, these thoughts, the shape
of waves, in this way come to rest,
from time to time, on the design
of your old India carpet.

I wade where you have gone barefoot.
I go into this room where you might come,
a desert. Walls breathe in the dark.
You cover every subject you love
with language, a latheworker oiling
the finished metal

cylinder, making it touchable again.
The prism you speak of is green.
You enter the hidden paths of it
so deeply lost in the lattice no one else
can see, the flame of your candle
claims the pages you write in heat
when you race out to eat.

When I enter any library, I know
how you could rest here, away from
the need to keep an easy flow of talk,
how bent on finding peace, your steps sound
solitary on the cool stone.

ii
I entered marriage as my parents dove together
in the surf, in that delight of some weight
lifted, as I entered the library
at the end of class. Peace would come
like that, a lifting in the chest,
familiar slant of light and scent, the knowledge
that the worst had been foregone.

In the library, reading your works
the peace came. It came every time
as it had come when I set my mother's table.

iii
Wedgewood flowers, red and blue
in porcelain basketweave,
the damask napkins folded.

And even now the grace of books and tables
brings me to the patience
I thought marriage carried,

the same settledness of beautiful
arrangements, words, numbers
falling into patterns and connections

that kept the blood on canvases
and out of the street,
color that kept the eyes of painters

trained on the fold of fabric,
ligament and religion,
how the vestments flowed over muscle

and the whole attentive being
of the artists moved over forms
as light comes to the eyes,

as life comes from all those painted
mothers. I saw liberty in being
like my nurses—loving children,

liberty in surety and trust,
the never wondering what next,
with whom, the men and women

so self-contained and affianced
as they approach the goldsmith saint,
Eligius, and with that look

of serious decision lean into each other
for their very lives.

iv

It would go, go right, go on. With closeness.
Forces of attraction powerful then,
especially. Fathers did not take mothers
from their newborn sons in rivalry.

Reading was not stopped by moving,
friendships by seduction and deceit.
Teaching was not cut off like breath
following the progress of someone else.

And consummation was wanted, O, it was
wanted as the integral brackets life
with the outstretched wings of a bird.
Everything followed, as light bent

and the senses carried information.
Do not the rays of light in falling
upon the bottom of the eye excite
vibrations which being propagated

along the solid fibres of the optic
nerves into the brain, cause the sense
of seeing? As clear as that, formed
open as a plate waiting for food,

the supplicant scallop shells my mother
filled with cream of fish and mushrooms.
Everything filled and was emptied
in enjoyment of the fullness. Everything

was a question with an answer that could
resolve as chords resolved a sequence
of other chords aching for such completion.
It was true, clear as the pull between us,

the need to alleviate distance to accomplish
trust. The fringed eyes of paramecia
in the microscope are no less clear,
and the grain on the oak desk I press this pen

across brings back the college writing rooms,
where I wrote of you. It was simpler then.

Marriages and calendars were the shaping form
of lives. Marriage was an ark and not a marathon.

v

This is college. Freshman year uncoils
like a cardiogram, gray scrolls, the arbitrary
cuts. Sleeping away from home, on the grounds
where I also go to school, I learn

time does this, winds like scales and columbines,
and holidays are octaves that resound
familiar intervals and weather. I leaf through
the reproductions of great painters I want to list

for the rest of my life. My life will be quiet
if I follow this course, this love of spacious
rooms and carefulness, the Art Library
where I work nights, watching over Reserve Books

doubled for demand, the Italians,
Panofsky's compilation, the Northern Painters.
I have forgotten, after all, the place where
the earthbound and the celestial lovers

stand. Bremen, I think, somewhere north,
the picture of the lovers with claws and greedy faces.
All hands grab at the bowls, at fruit, roasts, crusts
on the feasting board. No food reaches the mouths

and from the lips congealed blood drips,
the way it does from rabbits hung in village *boucheries*.
And in the other panel the same table, the same blue buildings
seen through the windows. Except the lovers this time

all have wooden spoons tied with heavy cord to their wrists.
The cord is slightly frayed, the brush strokes fine.
So bound, each husband feeds his wife, each wife her husband.
The sweet face of the bride on the right lifts toward

her husband's spoon. At the far left another groom
dips his ladle into a deep tureen, so carefully,
so careful the inward eyes, watching not to spill a single drop.
How astonishing that I am paid to watch over such faces,

to note the colors of devotion—the blue and red, the blood,
running, drawn from life, wounds, knives, swords,
hung turkeys, turtles, still-lifes, gobbets
of setting blood, and all aggression contained

in these folded garments red and blue
as arteries and veins.

vi
O, baby, red and blue, little sister,
wrinkled. Our mother did not love you
with your wrinkles. And I saw how she hid
sick and sicker. Red-purple splashed

the walls with smashed fruits. *It's a long way
to Tipperary,* Mary sang from County Cork,
sang to you in Irish while I built block
on block in the nursery chanting the alphabet.

I remember building, tumbling, building again,
the ordinary things. From dogs I knew already
the way our mother acted was not normal, even
for someone who had to have a boy. I built

cities and let laughter at the crash of toppled
towers, the harmlessness, carry me to relief.
I entered those lettered constructions
as I later entered the library, praying

for your safety. You were born late, girl,
as Newton was born early. And the mothers
who saved you both called you ugly, ugly,
a brown jug, our mother said, a quart jar, his.

Because they wished the best for you,
and saw how real life falls so far away
from hope. The babies in Duccio's paintings
looked so much nearer death, and gray.

vii
Or green. I was that, though I didn't look it,
green that freshman year, and not prepared
to have the women in a women's college love me.

La. In the hours gone to passion, bodies, touch,
I loved only men. Like any woman
of my time and place,

I was ready for play and
readier to punish myself
for ever saying no to need. So set myself

the task of learning French this well:
that I could write of books as easily as I loved.
And set myself the harder task of learning German

well enough to travel on my own. I went
to Germany and learned to leave language
to the air, hold women when they wept

at what the men they lost had done
and listened to them beg forgiveness
for the holocaust in railway cars

and chapels, museum halls and kiosks
in the cities. I looked like the slaughtered
lost, was called Anne Frank once, or maybe

more than that. *Sie sind Jüdin, nicht wahr?*
Und Sie sind so amerikanisch gekleidet.
As if they might for a splinter's instant

find relief for finding one of us alive
and willing to speak in their tongue
by choice and love in this century

of broken connections. Yes, I told them, yes,
my name is Sussman, Austrian, spoke in hushed
gutturals in their very churches, not unlike

the ones I went to daily with my Welsh governess.
Flow gently, sweet Afton, gently, she sang to me
all my growing up, sang often, and pronounced

it, as in always and often (a phrase she used),
like the river Afton, with a *t*. How is it
for you that I am here in church, where I

have often been? *Ich bin ein jüdisches Mädchen
und bin hier in diese Frauenkirche.* I went against
my parents' will, was set, could feel the ease

of knowing what came next and next, security
as mechanical as your laws, Newton, until
a man with the movie raincoat in a church, opened,

showed me all his glory, and I fled.
And did not think to find him in the marriage bed.

viii
Liberty lay there, as through the arched
entry hall of books, the certainty of stacks
and carrels, chapels, clocks and maps
of where to find periodicals, long tables
and the grained oak surfaces I loved

and leaned on, writing in lined notebooks
what I read between the lines and strokes.
I climbed secretly to the rafters and the campanile
with the girl who wanted, when we got there
among the mice and lung-shaped dusty pockets

of the hiding-place she had discovered, to know
if I knew *The Well of Loneliness,* and would
I please make love. O Newton, your reticence
and terror is like my stunned sorrow
at having to say no and try to hide

the fury I, too, felt, that she could think
to ask. And she was young and beautiful
and new. I've seen that murderous glint
of anger, brief as a splinter's entry
at being put in such a situation, seen it

as we walk casually in an afternoon, say in
a park, and talk of fences, daffodils
and signs. Fundraising friends extract
the negative from me with blushes still.
And Raising Cain or climbing anything—
the ladder for the casserole on the kitchen
corner shelf—I recall that chaste refusal.

ix
I did not mention it, nor spoke of the professor
who taught me physics that first year:
unchilded, she would call me afternoons to talk
of your work, so she could tell, before
retirement, tell without telling, the sorrow
of her life, unknown but palpable as the air,
and have me near her

in that loss. Her white hair almost blue
as Holbein eyes, her eyes that blue, her smiles
as seeming unaware as any member of my family
of rage and greed, as I was sure

of them, and sure they had to be contained
in paint and print, in sport and making love,
as engines move our journeying through difficult
terrain. Her voice as sweet as honeyed, thin

farina, careful as the sicktray it was carried on,
this woman asked me to read the *Opticks*
and *Principia,* so I could come discuss
the work with her those gargoyled

afternoons. No one misstep, mistake, no touch,
query, no irritable *I don't give a fig for
Newton, as you might have guessed,* only being
kept and kept in a brown room,

the absence of even tea,
and how she smiled and smiled
and kept her hope
alive and me at middle distance.

When I am tired now, I can hear your voice, Newton,
a Cambridge don before London
and the Royal Society, hear it in dulcet
deepness on my answering machine, crowded

out by other messages, dwindling, slowly
making me accept the vanishing

of hope, and I remember winter, small talk
about the *Principia,* talk like this of how
you would sound in person, and I feel
the old professor's held-back tears.

x
When I am tired now, my younger son
complains I have no conversation.
I am likely to be thinking it would
have made my life much sillier had
he not been born. There is no small talk
for such feelings, how I feel when he

performs not for glory but the sheer
delight of artists like my parents
together in the surf. Nights I come home
to his practical physics. He is juggling
oranges and beanbags, plastic pins.
This freezing nine o'clock, the back door

is wide open, snow gusting into costly
heated rooms. He is barefoot, sick with fever,
but standing at the cold shaft of air.
He holds a plastic wand and magenta jar—
bubblestuff. He blows, his face rapt
as choristers singing *Messiah. Get in!*

I do mean in. Come in, this minute, shut
that door, you're asking for pneumonia. Come!
I interrupt his passion, though I understand,
I think. In the small noise of snow
kissing linoleum, he has put a question
to the patio and finds flakes hit breath-driven

bubbles and do not break them but sit on them
and turn them around and around, until the globes
are coated and heavy and land and explode.

xi
Put out the light and then put out the light.
My older son, ecologist, has given me a candle
snuffer for my birthday. Brass butterfly

resting open-winged on the inverted cup,
the heft of this curved handle in my palm
moves to douse the flame, two flames,

as if the wrought butterfly would
take off after a brief moment
of such heat and rest and not return

though contained in this meadow
of some known breadth and depth.
As scientists catch tagged

Oenius chryxus in the mountains
of Colorado and let them go,
never thinking of Aeneas or of Christ,

trying to find how far they fly,
how often meet and mate and what
they feed on, we promise not to impede

the pattern of each other's lives
more than the instant it takes
this brass instrument to kiss

the moving flame. Like this
I want to say I love you; in such
fixity of hope and purpose,

such liberty of moving in these
ancient fields, their windows
of receding absence dance.

I move to where you are as dustmotes
travel on the slanting beam.
Newton, you are with me, gone.

xii
If I could tell you how the peace comes
some afternoons like weather
or a randy creature that has just
shaken loose its snow
from the charged and unknowing

atmosphere of waiting,
how even as it comes,
at evening,
the knowledge enters—
a sensation of wind on the lips,
drying them, until the tongue must

come to the rescue
with silver moisture and the silver
silence holds the rocking water
and the small noises of waves
lapping against the ribs
of ships and deprivation,
and the moment breathes generosity
and the humor that permits tears
and spit and semen to be grace itself,

if I could say this knowledge was simple
as the first kiss or arithmetic
and only means it will happen again
as one means the possibility
of another one, this brief ease
and rearrangement,
a room of furniture made larger
and more spacious by using
lost corners and hidden curves
in the bitterness of attrition,

if I could reassure you this settling
of satisfaction will come again,
still, you would not see
how even as you keep scarce
and I lose ground and do not
find paid work, my friends are
sending me letters, lending me
favorite books, feeding me apples
and grapes in winter and bread
their hands have kneaded,

even in this rushing press,
a century of words lost for thankfulness
and for rescue that is winding now

inexorably to its full complement
of zeroes. O, flow, gently,
sweet, often, join me in this song,
soon, now, and do not stare in such love,
blank with the barreling old torment
at the millennium
closing,
down.

Emilie du Châtelet: Notes Found
accompanying Her Translation of the Opticks

"Are not the rays of light
in passing by the edges and sides
of bodies, bent several times
backwards and forward
with a motion like that of an eel?
And do not the fringes of colored light
arise from three such bendings?"

Thirty-one queries you composed like this
as if we could say anything but yes to such
imagination. In the lacunae between clear forms,
the ground around known matter, your hope flowed.

"Gravity tends downward
but the pressure of water arising from gravity
tends every way with equal force,
and is propagated as readily
and with as much force sideways
as downwards, and through
crooked passages as through
straight ones.

   "But
    light
    is
never known
to follow crooked passages
nor to bend
in the shadow."

How much I want to add to what you know—that light,
so removed from touch, when passing by clear bodies
even the very rays of it cannot resist
a small caress,
and fingers of light reach,
for a brief moment
to flow around
the journeyers in its path.

How you wanted to travel like that,
follow on wings your mother
when she moved to leave you.

How you must have dreamed the bond would break
between the propagating bodies of that union,
dissolve,
release her back to you.
It went hard to watch those children being born,
the motions of that union
that distantly.
And after that you knew
all bodies are composed
of hard particles,
even the rays of light
seem to be hard bodies, you understood,
for otherwise they would not retain
different properties on their different sides
as a river carves an oxbow,
as strands of light move
on different paths through a prism.

Study keeps us through the long grief.
He does not want me any more.
In hours like this, the breeze moves
the curtains, and I think I could stay here
and he would want me back.

If we were trees
standing this way,
this close, our trunks
reaching straight toward the sun,
our branches would tend
toward the open space
on the far sides of each other.
Our leaves, being leaves,
would interfoliate
to enclose us.

Minds can do that
if speech has learned
to catch the senses in with sense.

Cow parsley, you say,
is that what this reminds me of?
Your nose dipped in the last fall flowers
from the garden. Breathing in many marigolds,
your cheeks grow dark
with the registry of time and scent

as skies at evening keep
the sun's stain. O, love,
the sight of your pleasure,

as you stand there alone,
fills me, rooted here,
with need, even as the fragrance
enters you, and you give words
to the pungent doubling.

Cow parsley. Marigolds. Trees.
There are no minds like leaves.
Whole lives are shaken by this reverberation.

To Newton: Of Light on Water

The colors of flowers in the dark, if we could see them,
would be tactile, moist, like a movie made for the blind.
They come like water
in the small hairs above the lips,
the droplets forming perfectly, without instruction
from the mist and labor of running
or walking in the heat.

And though I still fail to remember
how tired I get, and the thick, obstinate world,
how it beckons, like the dying, with chores to be done,
the untended sheds and cupboards
much more insistent in their silence
than the distant old, I rearrange shelves
as if order could fill in for loss.
The limits of time hedge me
clear as the privet I must trim and trim.

Though I can forget how much I need to hold back,
even the praise for those I love,
I visit this brick house where my sons live half their days
with their father, the new brother, sister, wife.
We are friendly, though the white dog sits half-lazy,
half-alert thumping its tail on the cool wood floors.
Thea her name, they say. A yellow labrador,
like a monkish polar bear, shaved sleek,
the whole body smooth as if once fur
hung in shaggy clumps. This cream-color could be
the ash of the living, neutral as envy that has spent itself,
a scene of impossibility, pearled ballgowns behind glass
in a museum: no one ever wore those clothes,
and loved, and danced, and laughed.
Here where the family grows,
I am dazed, as if bulbs I set one dark November
had come up somewhere else, on the far side of the garden,
and the lost island, Atlantis, raised its back lazily
as a dolphin resting from long play. I do not cry.

That guard dog guards. Orange poppies blaze
the delicate leather of their petals in a wide meadow,
and the sun makes chains of light
where water was.

II. OF PIERRE BONNARD AND HIS WIFE
AFTER THE BONNARD EXHIBIT,
THE PHILLIPS GALLERY, WASHINGTON, D.C., JUNE 1984

i
She is everywhere in this work, this wife
ageless,
written into the canvas, held in color
and meaning,
as Beatrice gone, Dante
wild with grief and loss
wrote from her,
as you, your mother gone,
gave your life to find
the drawstrings between
distanced bodies.

Sometimes I think I could guess
what absence Adam's rib stands in for.
And here she is, the answer to that agony,
presence more than solace, Eve.
There comes a thickening like summer air
about to give out dry, muddy rain
and then this color that seizes breath instead,
as if on the neutral wall the canvases were sky
tilted upright in shock at its own magnificence.

The light is too much for the heaviness of this marriage,
this woman caught in pain in paint.
It is permitted on such occasions
to love invisibilities as you did, or, as here,
a house, a field, a yard.

ii
Here I am inside these paintings,
inside another history like yours, set down in colors

brighter than the peacock's tail whose eloquence
in iridescence spoke to you. Those feathered eyes
do not outshine the greens and blues in these rooms,
and comets are no more silver than the steam
on these glistening tiles.

iii
Entre Deux Guerres

This is Le Carnet, 1928, war over, war not yet arrived.
The country home and fields in which it is set
are loved in these canvases
beyond the way light quickens the patio
and the shoulders of a woman.
She milks a cow, a child sprawled on the ground beside her.
The leaves and crops are streaks, green shoots and falling
stars in August.
The glass plates on the pink table hold silver.
Round as a woman carrying a child,
the glass pitcher holds water.
Some of it has been poured into a glass.
She how far away it is,
the woman carrying liquid in paint toward a man,
light on water in a transparent cup.
She is happy in this service, happy walking
from the French terrace
through the casual vines and flowers down.
She is moving with the raptness of an artist,
moving toward her purpose, the man, thirsty
toward whom she moves, as he,
the object of her quest in the composition, is given
to painting that moment, all of those moments,
this marriage.

iv
Here nothing is extinct. Shadow fish swim under the bathing
woman. Half-floating in all the connecting waters of the
world, she is safe.

Look at her nakedness. Look, dear. It cannot hurt you.
In these other paintings she is also bathing.

Or has just stepped out of the bath. Once, her husband
captured her at table, holding a dachshund
in something resembling fear and affection.

v
These are the moments for painting,
clear as the red-checked tablecloth, the squares where
white threads cross the red,
the moments where change occurs.

vi
This is not pink, this paler red suspended
between full color and full blankness, never empty.
After sleep and dream, the bed shared, the bodies held
in timelessness,
day, flesh, and the alarm of pulling apart for work
could take a lifetime to forgive.
The ripping, however slow, from that warmth
ripples shock and knowledge,
breeds the retreat at siesta back into merger and ease.
Languorous in daylight, having loved, the sleeper
is this man's wife. How he must have wanted
to keep her young, keep her there
against a loneliness, inevitable and necessary
as the pale green glass that bends light,
shows us its anatomy in a rain-drenched sky,
this nakedness we all come to.

To Newton: White, on Saint Augustine
Thinking Marriage Better Than Burning

I mean the wings of the egret opening like this on the marsh
this morning, opening and closing again, that whiteness,

the rush of will without blood, without grave risk,
like the Amazons who are said to have known the art

of piercing their breast with daggers, without bleeding.
That moment, just after the knife cuts through,

parting the flesh before color seeps into that fresh blankness,
the moment of a girl's puberty, before the knowledge of blood

that is not, after all, death. Do women, touching blood so often, have
less need for blood-sacrifice? We have our ways of knowing

the sky about to open some message of change or dread,
like a letter from you, the white envelope, that slight

slant of your cursive, my address. Last night
I dreamed of us and my hand, in sleep,

scored my arm reaching for you. I have skimmed
the whitest skin above my wrist in silence, taken

the plumb of your refusal along the surface. My dull nails
have left the red tail of a comet. Whenever the weather

is warm like this, and couples lean into each other,
and half the world wears white and breathing cotton,

I must fight off the clear picture of that ascent
in which the paired animals, astonished

at having been chosen, as if discovering they were
the separate lengths of white light that made the rainbow,

slowly walk the ramp you have turned away from.
They climb to the arc of safety.

To Newton: Of Saint Augustine and Snow Angels

*Now if we conceive these Particles of Bodies to be so dis-
posed amongst themselves, that the Intervals of empty
Spaces between them may be equal in magnitude to them
all: and that these Particles may be composed of other
Particles much smaller, which have as much empty Space
between them as equals all the Magnitudes of these
smaller Particles: And that in like manner these smaller
Particles are again composed of others much smaller, all
which together are equal to all the Pores or empty Spaces
between them; and so on perpetually till you come to
solid Particles, such as have no Pores or empty Spaces
within them. . . . And there are other ways of conceiving
how Bodies may be exceeding porous. But what is really
their inward Frame is not yet known to us.*
—Isaac Newton, the Opticks, *book 2, part 3*

i
It could have been like this:
One night we make *frangipane*
and it turns out smoother
and more golden than all the recipes hinted.
You find the roll of almond paste
in the freezer
for no reason we can think of
in the cabinet a bottle
of unopened Grand Marnier.
It's years and I'm still afraid
you don't remember how you beat
the eggs and milk to thickness
while I cheered *More, keep stirring, more*
like the dirty joke you told me
years ago. I think we both were laughing
when I pulled the old enamel saucepan
from the stove, laughing
so much I nearly dropped it.
You didn't scold my clumsiness for once
and we couldn't eat more than that
one spoonful each and said so.

65

And spread the butter just in time
to glaze the top before skin formed.
Remember? We went on talking,
idling over coffee about teenagers
and divorcees we knew who took the Pill,
that one telling you on the run
she kept resisting so what was the good,
the other, younger, telling me more or less
the same. I don't know what we had for supper.
We gave the kids ice cream and tucked them in
without a story, we were so hungry for richness
past their liking. You found the marzipan,
both of us amazed. I got out the cookbook,
milk, sugar, eggs. Not a scrap of chocolate
in the cupboard. And from those few elements
perfection. Both of us called it that,
and sat, unable to let go. I still see
your dazzled eyes. And sometimes think
if Augustine had been a woman he would have said:
Better to burn the custard than the marriage,
and not been joking. The way we tasted,
talked until you howled at me again
that I denied you everything and always had.
As if you could have eaten all the pudding
that same night. As if I wanted it
all to myself the rest of my life.

ii
Since then I am alone. In spring the dogwood
drops its petals, slow in their long fall
as cold, falling leaves. I think of snow,
snow like that, in spaces between trees
where the glare is gentled by the shadows.
I still can summon how feet feel steamed
in rubber boots, red, the cold appearing,
seizing toes, ears, noses, despite scarves
tied like some single letter to
the safe-keeping clouds: *I am here,* an X,
in red or green stripes.

And so much noise.
The screaming field and playground do not seem

like din, then, all that steady holloing
comes in when we are older.

Snow angels I have photographed in full silence
like mystifying shadows of the trees,
dwarfed and mocking as bonsai
or a distorting mirror in a fun house at a fair.

If trees could laugh at these reflections
at their base in winter
we would have company in nature.
Nothing laughs that's not aware
of paradox and possibility.

Hypotheses that fit facts but could not happen,
like the Resurrection in a helicopter,
are always laughable.

And what I want to say about imagined things
is how we all, like scientists and artists,
throw ourselves like children in the snow,
into the knowing
of the tree in winter
or the woman's solitude,
the man's ambition answered
and his fear of being bound to sameness
all his life.

That giving up of who we are,
the getting lost and entry
that avoids the obvious walls and weight and density
that keep us out
turns tyrants into parents
and lovers into partners for their lives.

Confluence of need binds us
only for a moment, unless the slow, long press
of curiosity guides us
to know the snow as it is marked, but not claimed,
by the impression of the angel's shadow
left in the concave bas relief,

how it sinks and flattens,
how it yields and keeps, and disappears.

iii
We cannot be colonial in love.
And for all women I have ever talked with
C. P. Snow left too much out of his description.

There are only men and women and different adaptations
to the panic and terror of not-knowing.
People, and their many cultures, approach
what is not familiar
and the loss of attachment
in different ways, and language,
and gesture, and training, the structure of thought itself
shape those entrances to grooves.

Objectify embrace, Professor Snow.
Put your substantial heft into the crystal bed that hillsides wear,
your namesake, and listen to what it tells you—
the fine sound
a million openings kissing in the compression
the bones of their arms and legs crushed
bearing your weight.

iv
Newton, did you try not to be afraid?
The year my friend's brother died at eighteen,
her father had fallen from the window where he stood.

We went behind the Natural History Museum
and built enormous rounded figures in the snow
reclining in that court where the dogs walked

like the royal couple on sarcophagi I only saw years later
carved by the Etruscans and preserved in the Villa Julia
in Rome: a man and woman alive to each others' warmth

we molded of good-packing city snow.
Shy, even blushing, but not stopped by all the passersby
who came to watch and asked where we went to art school,

we smiled and, as I recall, said nothing,
like our melting alter egos in the sun. In loss,
I fill the silent troughs with substance thick as snow,

with edge enough to make crystals prickle skin, dart
to the center of the hurt in answer and a kind of proof.
It is. I feel this way. We never spoke of those deaths, she and I.

It would have been too much. We carved progenitors
to make new life, parent statues melting together, neither,
left to live and die alone. We walked her dog and learned

to drive and slammed the ball along the length of many hockey
fields between us, she center, I left inner or right wing.
And if I had the right paid work, I could be easy in this life

in an open frame, married with a man I only see
when we both have liberty enough, each having friends
and the faculty of speaking wittily enough and true

and clear, to avoid blame. I didn't want more than
reciprocity and a field wide enough for play from any man.
And need to give the same. Looking some days at the young

in amazement that makes me blush and breathe fast
waiting at the Stop sign where some Adonis jogging
in fine warm rain passes, his nylon Olympian decolleté

clinging to the edge of his long, moving legs,
tendons rippling, nipples clear through net as pendant
genitals cradled in the sweat-drenched shorts,

hands combing through the air, I would like to laugh out loud
at the healthy spectacle and call something idiotic
from the car: *Want a ride home?* spoken to a self-contained,

directed man, looking ahead and in no need of company,
budding and building to whatever he does need for answer
and accompaniment. That's when I know, if Augustine

had been a woman, or Paul himself, and written from my station
we would have kept devotion in coupling and not have so
misshapen marriage. If the form were only a reflection

of the curiosity I cannot help but feel for the few I care
about this much, the compassion following like a veil,
vows and promises, the awesome injunction of the long arc

of a lifetime would seal and not constrain. It seems to me
the harking back to what is already there between
makes a union, the seizure of the future in prediction kills.

O lord, if the sweet bliss confirms promises and the worst
we do is keep each other waiting, there must be room for pairs.
Newton, we live still by needing to know and move.

Domination is just another version of defense against change
and truth. Which does not mean it is not meat and drink
to half the world. In courage, I want to know, don't you?

In fear I want to destroy fear which means the other one,
everything not like me, or everything I do not like.

v
And I don't know if they do this in England,
or where, except the Cotswolds,
there might be full snow, there, then,
when Newton lived, or now.

But any child not terrified of scolding
for wet or muddy clothes
might think of flight
and fling this body safely to the cushioned ground
in winter
snow
so like a pillow in the dark
the white even dimmer
than the stars
left on the lids of closed eyes.
Snow like that, remember? in the spaces
between trees, where the glare is gentled
by the memory of falling petals.

vi
In any case, a pillow is not snow
and children are not angels

70

but snow angels is the name we give it here
this side of the Atlantic
when children give themselves
to the gesture of sure lovers
and lie down
and spread their arms and arc
the full-feathered, gloved fingers up and down
like wings. The pattern is very like

old pictures of the angels
or the paper carvings
sentinel and crown of trees at Christmas
in the houses hung with flakes of snow
and those where light is heralded,
with amber candles that reflect
burning oil and the flames of silver stars.

In any case, there must be love in marriage
full and strong at the center as a child in snow, tumbling,
leaving the mere impression in the shell.
There must be love at the center, and liking,
and the amusement of hillsides. I have heard
a saying around the schoolyard this year:
when angels have lost everything
they go out in the snow
and make children.

To Newton: On Snowflakes

In effect, a snowflake records the history of all the chang-
ing weather conditions that it experiences.
—The New York Times, 6 January 1987

Have you entered the storehouses of the snow, or have
you seen the storehouses of the hail,
which I have reserved for the time of trouble, for the day
of battle and war?
What is the way to the place where the light is
distributed, or where the east wind is scattered upon
the earth?
—Job 38:22–24

Some nights alone like this with snow falling
outside my window, I listen to the small sound
of kisses, see the earth as mouth and womb receiving
this lawn of milky blooms.

We can see them now, the storehouses of the snow,
how the droplets gather from a mere suggestion
in the air and crystals chronicle each shift
in weather and surround.

They are not symmetric, quite, each branch
slightly different, and still
more like the other prongs of its own longing
than any arm of any other flake.
Yes, we are many selves, six at least, some existential
snowflake might proclaim, *each individual as you,*
or you, each spirit another story of matter
in time and weather, keeping to the pattern,
crocheted tablecloths, lace. In this white garden,
without genetic code, the responsiveness of growing seeds
is real and metaphor for souls, I half suspect. How
in the deep of each of us, nature interacts

with nurture to keep variety. The crystal stair, cocoon,
and sun and storm mean this: there are no clones.
Newton, you feared that gathering in the sky of you,
preferred the stability of the great swirls of galaxies,

the long, measured temperance of stars, as if God
entered the dark and spilled the fertile seeds
of fire and light, once or twice, for nanoseconds
lapsed to fountaining.

And we peer up at that expression in the sky, spume,
and semen, milk or frozen joy. We peer up as I peered
as a child at an X-ray in my father's office,
a large black film hung high, holding the lit bones.

Even now in this weather, I open to hope
and pray against centuries and likelihood
you did search some winter's nights,
yearned after the fullness and furthest

reaches of yourself, summoned the longing that joins us
—creatures not beasts—
across emptiness, across time.

To Newton: Of Ivory Beads

The half-moons of my nails
whitened with a wet white pencil,
this early morning tending in the first light.
I wonder in such quiet if you liked to watch
the dawn come, that lightening without lifting.
This morning I know God's nails were never dirty
from tending the earth. God has no clock.
It's 5 A.M. and the light comes through the dark,
breaking it up like a fight between brothers.

And how that pink comes out of the black
and makes the sky pinched in winter
like a maiden aunt who has lived too long
with a dachshund and deprivation,
how I have turned back to white sheets
after all the patterned years, new sheets
white as paper, whiter than white,
those words I tried to understand when I was small.
People called the hair of grandparents white
when it was yellow and ivory, and the ivory carved
beads my mother did not wear but let me hold
were the white beads. But soap and clouds

and the pure truth chalk spoke on the blackboard
were whiter than hair. In this light, I begin
to remember the mystery. Whitest of all
were the aprons Agnes wore in the warm kitchen
of childhood, and the smell of her ironing,
scalded linen and damask, napkins never burned,
made thick with folds, whole tablecloths brought
to order like sails stored in a harbor, white
in her knotted, spotted, wrinkled hands I loved
and hardly noticed then.

To Newton: In the Museum of Natural History

An hour to kill in the city and I come here
to these vast halls, my woods when I was small
for roaming in. Here teeth and feathers, insides made
transparent

and bloodless.
These clocks in trees, for instance, the stone thrown
and time ripples water for a thousand years.
This giant redwood began in 482 A.D., the teacher reads

from the placard.
In the dim room, her command is genetic: *Copy that!*
And the students asked to inscribe in speckled notebooks
this date and the Latin for redwood are saying out loud:

Is this a tree?
The upended platter on the wall gives off light—
your face after three hours of talk, the bark
your hair in chunks at the end of immersion.

I love you
and these halls I search are only packed with strutting
kids in jeans, wielding combs, swishing brushed hair.
The little ones hold hands, follow their feet, afraid

to look so high.
Their teachers hurry them along like molecules grown
cold in some experiment. "Now move, Brian, move. Jenny, walk!"
Everything is off-scale here. These rings echo like sadness

bringing tears.
Preservation is an emblem for distance, Newton. And dryness.
What's close dies, gradually, or in violent throes.
This week I've been attentive to the mushrooms, leeks, and carrots

I chop for soup.
Their shapes and surfaces take my breath like a long,
wanted kiss. We don't accuse trees, with their concentric
rings, or animals of the compulsion to repeat, that reaching

back to get it
right again or for the first time, late. The buttons
of the TV cable unit are arranged like teats. Any hour
my mother cat will turn them on by leaning hard

legs under belly
where once her kittens tugged and purred. And when I hold
her consort to me, his eyes moving across my face,
when I lift him from the cavern of the dryer he crawls into

even as I lift
the clean, warm laundry to the folding place, when I see
how he investigates, how the seeds at the center
of his eyes are like the shape of every cell

that seeks to grow
I know again how much I needed to come close
to the warm-eyed seals I could not stroke in childhood,
the walrus on far rocks I longed to lie with, if they

would have let me in
documentaries, even the manatees I still watch in nature
films. And why the black fur of my father cat is not wet,
I sometimes can't imagine as he looks at me with such eyes

or if purrs come
from trying to talk with the sea. I know it is good
to find answer, the tumble of appetite, like the great redwood in the
    museum,
a slice of what once lived,

its mosaic
center grown in the time of Byzantium, the seed entered,
sprung then, that long ago, to green. When I remove my father
cat from every new dark place he nosedives into

I remember
all I wanted was to tend these surfaces in love, knowing
the familiar new each morning, and the children, like prayer,
or any lover, him I missed, carrying what I cannot lift

laundry today
down the narrow stairs. He comes to me, as I to him,

when we cry *here, help, here,* like any seed in the ground.
And so move through the absences together all our lives.

The slice of leek
I saved out on the white formica yesterday had small green
bands like ridges on a tide-marked scallop shell marking
time like ancient calendars. It spoke of repetition,

your return,
that axis of desire that aches for unsurprise,
the clear knowing that comforts us in the dark. Toes
and fingers grope at the edge of things like telescopes

adventuring
in galaxies and finding grit and thirsty clams.
Another hour we drink, another rim of glass. We round these
familiar seasons, exchange stories of strange journeys,

getting lost.
Just now, a naked woman, breasts, nipples, uterus and all,
ovaries ready to explode the nautilus spiral of her fallopian tube, a
    seed about to
join, grow, navigate,

root, reach seeking,
a stone thrown to a pool. She is plastic, I parched.
O Newton, in this basement, I can see you rush,
your years of reaching to touch only distance

become eyes
searching these naked figures science serves behind glass
plates. Would they, more than the curves of Sivas
from old India, or Michelangelo catching need

and health and God
in ligament and torsion of a body stretched by an idea
have moved you? Curiosity keeps apart from trust.
As you won't hold me, I can see you trying not to look,
racing these halls,
your head turned despite resolve, your hands trying not to touch the
    glass.

To Newton: On My Purse
and the Dryness of the Heavens

You could be watching me open this purse,
watching me hunt the key that will open

the doors to paradise, the key a plastic card
in my wallet, buried at the bottom under

pens, barrettes, lipstick, glasses, papers,
perfume, comb. Yes, you are watching me perform

this surgery, all the organs entangled
as lovers. Just five minutes ago, you were

watching the second hand on the watch I wear.
Your eyes found my high heels. They make such noise

on the marble floors. This is an official hall,
entryway to the natural history of the universe,

and you are watching the soft plums I carry
near my heart. I am breathing hard,

trying to find the card, the key, hit that one
mark, answer, and you are watching this crowded

tumble in my hands, this earth, its passion,
grounded, puffs of tissues I might need

for the wetness of this labor, the water
that is nowhere in the long burn of that sky

you touch.

To Newton: About Hertz, Purring, and My Cats

Those who lecture regularly tell me they dream even now,
after many years of experience, they are standing naked
before the audience, their ignorance and everything else
exposed. I who do not speak often at public gatherings wake
to dreams of telling a distinguished group of men and women

the most ordinary things. This morning I have not done
the dishes, left them in the sink and used the coffee filter
a second time. I know nothing about gardening, I am saying,
but the generations of landlessness in my family handed down
ways of walking fearlessly enough in city traffic.

I am a professor of daily life and they, this audience,
are interested. They look attentive. I am naming the virtues
of setting home clocks ten minutes fast. I rarely miss buses
anymore, I have a few minutes to devote to waking up from dreams
like this. The audience, I can see, is expectant, wanting

the real subject of my lecture. I seem to know there is
something we can agree on, those of us who love dailiness
and the way life will go on, if the killing stops. I have been
persuaded for so long, the more I find out, the more I am moved
by mystery. There is astonishment in seeing likeness

in the least likely combinations. Just last week in the newspaper,
a cross-section of a brain cell looked exactly like a tree
in the old high-school textbooks, xylem and phloem. Current flows
both ways in any dendrite. That was the news. Until last year,
the scientists assume the signals moved in only one direction.

Mystery does not inhere in ignorance, I am saying. How much
information is packed that carefully in so intricate and unseen
a bundle and the number twenty-three, like the best gold, and all
the amino acids in the world. The crystal of our being holds two
football teams, the ball, and all the substitutions and the plays.

The sun is heating up the room in which I speak.
I squint at the late warmth. Ropes of dustmotes
stretch from the high windows to my right, the west,
as I face the audience. I am saying my male cat, father of these last
kittens I promised my children before they leave home, the male cat,

contrary to all the books I have read about mammals, lies with his
consort and their offspring, like graylag geese and other bonding,
partnered birds. He is licking the small gateways of the kittens.
There is no shame in waste among the animals I know best, only
discretion. The father has grown fat during this pregnancy.

He helped his mate deliver their kittens. He comforts them
with his tongue and tends their mother while she feeds
the toothlessness and hunger, the round ears growing until they
    point
the eyes open, the legs strong. "People deserve their pets and
    children,"
my landlady claimed in Cambridge. And I spent that British year

in your city mortified my inventive children would cause eviction.
    They did not
use their crayons on her walls. These six cats sleep a whole season
in my open bottom drawer. I take no credit for their kindliness.
And wish I did deserve such living emblems of my dreams of enduring
affection, factories sweet as the vessels of the body. See how

the green things wait to breathe what I cannot keep. Answering.
Responsive. We speak in labor and creation, and I have heard,
even when we think we are silent, our smallest muscles give out
a low hum, like a purr our dull ears can't record. The frequency
of that inner voice is 23 Hertz, matching our paired chromosomes.

Some mystery is held in such resonance, the scales of things
so small and echoing, only the pathways of exchange sing the news
as a clock chimes on a rainy day.

To Newton on the Hardness of Bodies:
Gall Bladder Removal following the Death of a Turtle

i
"Have you any questions?" he asked,
the surgeon so elegant I could hardly look at him,
let alone look without images of desire's gentler
incision and insertion surfacing,
the surgeon, in my readiness so appealing,
I had to wonder, not infrequently, if abstinence
had made my body manufacture
another cause and site of entry,
asked me, even as I yielded to drugged surrender:
"Any questions?"

And of course even in that condition I asked,
because I had lately heard
there is a straight and narrow middle way in
between the ribs, the trunk of the tree
and an asymmetric cut beneath the right breast:
"What kind of incision will you make?"
"A lovely one," he answered, and I went laughing
out like calm moonlight on a lake.

ii
The cotton weave blankets are *this* soft
and bleached *this* white: I covet them
like those in my grandmother's house in summer
how they hold in their immunity
to astringents and their openness
the suggestion of hammocks, cradles, babies
about to arrive, weddings, and thanksgiving
tables, veils, feasts, lace.

It hurts to yawn.

The stones, sealed in a vial with my name,
are mottled, brown and green
in bas relief
as on a tortoise carapace—
two of them the size of grapes
the very shape the dim sonogram outlined.

"Now if compound bodies
are so very hard as we find
some of them to be,
and yet are so very porous,
and consist of parts
which are only laid together,

the simple particles
which are void of pores,
and never yet were divided,
must be much harder.
For such hard particles,
being heaped up together,
can scarce touch one another
in more than a few points,
and therefore must be separable

by much less force than is requisite to break
a solid particle whose parts touch
in all the space between them,
without any pores
or interstices to weaken their cohesion.

And how such very hard particles
which are only laid together
and touch in only a few points,
can stick together, and that so firmly
as they do, without the assistance
of something which causes them
to be attracted
and pressed toward one another
is very difficult to conceive."

God grant me liberty and keep me here
and alive, together in all my elements,
you cry between the lines. As I do
from these hospitable white sheets.

iii
Newton, the new equipment registers vital signs in lights,
numbers appearing round and slow, 95.3, 95.4
on the screen eking out a normal temperature

like a young child learning to write.
The waiting nurses hold the mounting numbers.

They are so patient I try
to memorize hair styles so I can tell
the difference between them. Their kindliness
comes with trim figures, clear skin, deft hands.
Trish prettiest, Elaine who shot me full of painful Mefoxin.

I could be an old woman
unable to stand straight.
I am entering the concrete
more every hour.

Old lessons about nature,
vacuums, and sucking water
to start the flow through siphons
have new applications here.

I could be a bivalve
an ordinary oyster
not wanting these large, brown pearls
irritants I have ground to tweed perfection
in the oyster-shaped cradle
of my liver.

It hurts to laugh.

The woman who wipes the floor is cheerful.
Her nameplate says: TINA: ENVIRONMENTAL
SCIENCES. She is concerned about my window,
sprays ammonia blue on the expanse of cloudless sky.
It makes me cough.

Coughing hurts
more than yawning
less than true laughter.

I had to hang up on my friend
who makes a joke of everything.
This one was about rabbits
and I, as we say,

cracked up.
I could see

perfectly

the real crack widening with the fire of that pain.
I am in stitches, I said to myself,
but even wit did not stop the laughter.
I almost fainted.

iv
I am trying to understand how, according to
quantum theory, everything is connected,
lazily, without cause and effect.
I am reading, as the anesthesia haze recedes, poems
and popular physics. I am trying
not to be jealous of the poet who had the marriage
I always wanted.
The poet tells of three days of desire with her husband,
satisfied, their shared and spoken grief at
an abortion they could not safely avoid.
But the words are not the feeling of desire.
Grief is not blood.

I speak to no one of this.

Everything forbidden is forgiven here, and wanted.
Belches, bleeding, bowels, farting, forgotten
periods or early, occasioned by surgery.
With such acceptance, you would not think
there would be competition
for I.V. poles and clean nightgowns
with blue snowflakes,
for Ed, the nurse with the songs.

"A straight line on a curved surface is a curve, or arc,"
the physics text says. The scar, after all, is moon-shaped
and smiling when I get around to looking at it from above,
two days later than I might have dared.
Nothing but the way the broad band of muscle, the diaphragm
which draws breath protests the door cut into it, jerks

and makes me cry out without warning is as startling
as the instruction to, forgive me, fart.
The night before

I had to come here, I dreamed
there was no moon.
It had exploded into fragments
and so, gone wild in a way all the nurses
and interns found perfectly coherent
and amusing, the humorous surgeon
removed my brain instead
for an implant in the sky.

v

Through three buildings and many unnamed
corridors, my tall, younger son traveled alone
to find my room the first day
he could get away early from school.

When he reached me, I was just walking
and he did not balk
at pushing the I.V. pole down the hall.
Without children I might not have come this far at all.
My body, like justice, made one large stone for each son,
sweet tokens of their internal passage in my
country, and gravel enough, the surgeon said, to make the path
of all their traveling beyond.
They both confirmed their faith:
I would surely die.
The older said he would stay away entirely afterward,
the waiting was so hard, the will to keep at work at school
so strong. They talked about summer
camp and falling backward blacked out
in someone's arms. The older came to visit when he could
and let his brother lead the way through all the corridors
of hidden blood.

Baseball was the only language they had for their fear
when they saw me alive.
They put you out, Mom, out.
They put you out.

Just last summer, after a swim, I saw them
for the first time in six or seven years,
naked, penises thick and sudden, crowned
in the wide nests of hair.
In such dusk, July,
I tucked this same tanned skin,
scabby knees and boysex of each of them
into the last pajamas with blue bears,
red trains, heat like this

meaning bottoms to bed, no tops.
It happened by accident—
maleness sprung from me,
and seeing it, again—
a whale on the horizon,
the enormous presence altering the water
for miles.

They stand here and I feel again
in this place matter is the issue, flesh the heart
not ideas though
half of what is being treated
can only be known by indirection
because of limited perception,
boundaries and walls,
things unknown
uncertain until arrived at
by breaking through.

This sounds like quantum mechanics,
except for the pain.
We are here to learn what is the matter, wrong,
we say, what is wrong?
We mind what is the matter

with the altogether carnal
making it right again
by what is left behind and whole
if possible, by art, in spite of gaps
we heal by hands, by heart.

In this place, blood is practical
and not such a beautiful color it makes you

draw breath, draw carefully
write instead of laughing
when breathing hurts the core
where the heart beats more hope,
more hope, more.

vi
I am alone again on a distant, empty corridor at night.
A solitary man in ordinary clothes appears.
This is the first time in all my growing up
taken in such a configuration I am certain
I am safe from rape.
What joy can there be for a violent man
in the easy spill from the newly sewn?
I know. I know.

I have entered the concrete.
And in this small shift to fearlessness
and the ordinary world
if the masking tape holds
around the storm windows of the back door
these weeks my neighbors feed the cats,
if the cats don't get lost in the storm sewers
where they go to keep warm and explore,
if the glass doesn't shatter because the masking tape holds,

and I forgive myself for not putting it on the old, warped windows,
exactly square, if the cats survive the coming cold
and lack of attention, and my sons come home,
if they forgive this bent, aching walk of their mother
they would have playing with more than words,
if the stitches remain firm and then dissolve as intended,
and I retain the details of hang-gliding Ed has
so carefully and casually left behind,
if I can forgive myself for not waxing the kitchen floor
before I left and someday understand
how some people's spice jars never get greasy,
how they shop for two grades of rice,
one for important guests, the other for the rest of us,
if the importance of keeping this cyclamen, chrysanthemum,
and begonia sent by this many friends alive
through all the coming winters of my longing
does not diminish though they die,

if I can look again at that day the turtle was hit on the road
and car after car hurled it like a weighted ball,
until I wept and turned my car and stopped the traffic
till I gathered that large, mutilated stone, domed
and dappled like these, in a blue bag I found in my trunk
wrapped the massacre and buried it in a running brook
and spoke words to it and the Native American dead
who believed this earth is carried
on the back of the patient creature
the blinded conqueror killed again and again,
if I can look at these stones
greeny-brown as that once-living animal
and not remember, once,
the carelessness of the road that day,
and not remember the care of these nurses
and my friends, I will have entered the concrete
as surely as the surgeon took his knife
and coolly cut my flesh to save
such common, necessary throughts.

.

III

epithalamion
(of freedom, marriage and the unified field)

To Newton: Proem—
After the Coincidence of Lightning
and the Dream of Holding You

After the dream of knowing it was you in my arms,
the shoulders real as oranges
after a midweek marketing,
after being certain we were together at last,
waking up, the quick
disappointment, the lightning
cracking, just then, the dark sky.

After I drank the coffee alone, again,
and went on
I wondered how I might tell you if I could:
look at the thing needing to be done,
I wanted to begin.
It is only a child running away
from home, when it is time. Look,
even Psyche, that most beautiful woman,
doubted her sisters, when they said
love observed is a beast. And she was proven
right. The dazzling beauty took her breath away,
and shook her hand. A drop of oil that had been light
burned her lover's cheek.
In the new story the husband
is a human carrier of love and hope and power, like us,
vulnerable as any sleeping child. We are all
at liberty in fierce attachment,
ready to wander the world for decades
to heal each other, separately, find each other again
where there is this much devotion, the kind that made
Eros and Psyche, the kind of dedication that made them
gods.

If only I could tell you, I would,
the joining is, after all, beautiful,
as Psyche is beautiful, only the looking might be wrong,
at first, like the tasting of the apple
in the other story, punishable by shame. But it is time,
clearly, we are meant to see it like this,
know it like this, we are meant to

be clean inside it, feeling it, even as we are seeing it,
we are meant to
shake like children caught
in the downpour, the center of the turning staircase
lit with stars,
the summer rain.

To Newton on the Form of Questions:
Randomness in the Universe

i
The way this one is born blind,
and that one is hit broadside,
the way the cellist loses her
ability to play when her muscles
are seized with M.S., and the composer
goes deaf, and the lover loses everything.
We say this is the luck of the draw.
I had a friend who could say: *better him than me,*
speaking of Beethoven, the talent and the curse.
And while I count my blessings more accurately
than my income, rejoice in, for example,
the lift that comes of rounding certain bends
in the long road home from work
with the music rising to the occasion,
still, sometimes the harmonies are so pure
tears come, tears for things not to do, now,
with me, so much as the remembrance of the cellist
unable to play, of the way your father could not stay
even for your birth, and your mother had to leave
you when you were three. Tears in the falling,
sunlight blazing off bare branches for various children
who have died, the friend who cannot bear to
watch just this, the falling sun from her picture
window. *How quickly it goes,* she says.
The quickness itself too sad now.
She is fighting cancer
with a brave voice and the best conversation.
A pair of dice, dammit, is not
a paradise.

ii
My eyes still do tricks when I cry in the light,
rainbows from the salty drops hung on the lashes
like an optical grid.
And, yes, there is a kind of pleasure, thus,
in crying, aesthetic
in someone like me,
not based on liking pain.

In the shuttered light, I can see you longing, too, as
I long for my lost hope.
Without you there is sometimes nothing.
And can I scatter small parcels of explosion
like stars given to the night, I who need a place
to come home and these beds of connection
more familiar, more curious than a key,
and the carved door
opening in darkness
to your silver?

Every question is an opening.

And what if there were daughters?
Would they have built round rooms in the sandy soil
when their brothers shaped cypress from the earth?
And do our words do tricks when we shine the light
on them? And is there an invisible silent half
of everything we know, for every sister who wins
a sister or a brother lost or dead
to make a whole we cannot comprehend?

I last saw my little sister at the beach.
High up on the sandy palisade,
we huddle together under one towel,
the grit between our thighs,
the sky more terrible than the sea,
as we watch our parents drown together.

Swallowed in the surf,
broken apart in the valleys between
waves, further and further their heads
and waving hands:
they choose this.

I could still carve
the shape of the precipice we guard,
the stretch of brown beach
before the sea begins, the breakage
slow and heavy of the overhang
dropping in parcels when a big wave comes.
We do not dangle our legs.

Watching back to the time
before my sister left
I try to understand
by what device my parents climbed
the ten-foot ledge
or rode a wave
straight into the crumbling wall
spilled over the top to us
alive
at the last moment.
Newton, what happens to us if we do not see our parents in delight?
If our mother was a daughter, unadored?
Tell me then where fancy lies?
In the cradle where it dies?

To Newton: Of Death and Eros,
John Milton and His Wives

Those to whom evil is done do evil in return.
—W. H. Auden, "September 1939"

For every action there is an equal and opposite reaction.
—Isaac Newton, *Third Law of Mechanics*

i
My word! here in the bed, John Milton
is much discomfited, with his several
wives *in seriatum*, disobedient.

He is playing *Samson Agonistes*, his strength
and blindness waging war inside his tent.
The wedding canopy has become the khaki

raincoat of the exhibitionist. He stands
with polished shoes gleaming on the foot
of the bed above one of his attending

wives. Let's guess the first. She, lying
in decorous soft curves, might be cowering.
He stands above her eyeing for an instant

her soft nightgown pale as butter. He looms
large, stage and actor now, curtains of the coat
parted to display his enormity. He smiles.

Says: *I am wonderful, don't you think?*
Sir Richard, here, my smaller wonder.
I love to show it you. Don't move.

Don't do a thing. Read this manuscript
of manly contest I've just writ. Let's
draw this out, this tunnel through

the river's heart and out the other side.
Liberty. I believe in liberty. And every
custodian of the traffic wants the flow

free to the other highway. Your hand please.
Touch this horse-driven chariot, the most
expensive wood, the gleaming brass.

Be still, I said. Shut down your voice.
You are not here. Only eyes and ears,
only sighs and no desire of your own.

I am glory. You are admiration. Come feel
the God in me you lack. In this act
there is no need. My very gaze is known

to cut the path I travel. I am in control.
Idiot. Stop. Lie still. Bronze bowl.

ii
Obey. Or I will cut you off
without a scent or minute
of regret, I'll get you going,

packing, dying for the trip
and then I'll take you
where the stars go, Acapulco,

Paris, Crete, I'll find
the cheap hotel, cockroach
and seediness not for romance,

my sweet, but dinginess to stop
the least note of pleasure
in your throat. Joy has no part

in this conversation. Delight
is beside the point. Power is what
desire is, will, wife, accomplishment.

I care what I have to say, my laws
are prelude to your promised keen applause.

iii
O Newton, I am so grateful to you
for fleeing from such torture of another,

there, though a woman, full of hope and soul.
It moves me that your celibacy, however
querulous, went all to measured words
and flew in balanced weights and pairs.
I would have liked to gentle you and make you whole,
sturdy as shoes mated for life, like birds.

On Translating Newton: Emilie du Châtelet to Voltaire, 1745

Today, I have been walking to the forking
brooks again, and, coming home, strayed,
in mind, to see les Halles again, Genève,
the confluence they have seen fit to name
La Jonction. It was, as always, the slower,
browner Rhône entering the greener Arve
like a diviner's branching rod, but so much
motion. I did not go for tumult, a momentary
frisson of desire, and I am quite aware,
and even smiling as I write, it may be
the other way around, the Arve slow brown,
the Rhône swift green. I smile at how, till now,
you would make sport of me, and how impatient
you would grow, knowing that denotative lapse
in me amounting nearly to a habit.

I can see the place so clearly, even when
I lose the names. How old are these currents?
The cliffs and deep green growth? I stood
above that joining in the park where we have
often walked and thought of being wanted again
like that, as those two rivers flow together
pleasantly, as if drawn because they choose
to be together—a puff at the point of union,
the water rises, starts back like a rearing horse
and then moves on again. Less white. Fewer
threads and bubbles in the corded flow.
It is not smooth as far as my eye can see.
Looking south, the surface is more like a rope
than a bolt of cloth, all that carved
water rumbling. I thought, or fancied,

as the English say, it carried words: *Accept,
accept*. O, love, I cannot. We are so many arms
and legs in urgency. And strange this dozen
years with you, in our cobbled courtyard,
the shelter I always feel entering from the street,
or, conversely, as you enter, that sequestering
which is a kind of hiding. Making love, how
the sounds diminish, as in sleep or diving

under water. It is always sudden, the coming through
those gates. And it was curious to attempt
such closeness in exile, despising, both of us,
constraints and fixed laws on human endeavor,
in exile for believing in liberty, even as we insist
on it, sitting alone, together, you with your
philosophy, I with my translations. Fixed laws

belong to things. Which, as you know—
and this I still believe and trust you have seen
faithfully in me—is why I embrace Newton.
Also why I have left you free of the embarrassment
of feeling bound these several years. Shall we
try again? The monkishness without conclusion
or inclination from your side for reprieve is
breaking me. I can feel each drop of what I am inside
tending toward the junction and I will not force you.
We may do as nature cannot: run the course the other way,
the river together in fullness and then, for no reason
but a knot at the center, some obstruction we will not
take the time to undermine, choose to diverge.
It has cost me more tears than I care to measure.
Be natural, I want to cry at you. Listen to Newton.

"The waves on the surface of stagnating water,
passing by the sides of a broad obstacle
which stops part of them, bend afterward
and dilate themselves gradually into the quiet
water behind the obstacle. The waves, pulses,
or vibrations of the air, wherein sounds
consist, bent manifestly, though not so much
as the waves of water." Age, or is it another,
younger woman has claimed your surrender.
And you will now be quiet in whatever it is
you suffer. I want your comfort. Lovers do.
From comfort new love rises. And clear work
you value no more than I. That sounds solemn
as a priest. And, indeed, I have been dreaming
of being wanted again in the Académie to lecture

on Newton's laws, Madame du Deffand eating
her heart out along with all the other gossips

because she thinks my passion for the simple
fixities that bind celestial bodies and not
lovers, even as affectionate as we, is only
pretention. As if science had not become
my steadying practice, and curiosity my proof
of bonding. *I must know. I care to know*
what is most unlike me, to know it and not destroy
it, neither it, nor me. Is the Rhône destroyed
to the south of La Jonction? The Arve? All rivers
in the sea? How do the small germaines of us
blend in our children? Do my brown eyes destroy
his green in our daughter? You never wanted
children. Standing above that dense water today

the awful thought of entering its alien indifference
filled me with dread. I knew death for whole moments,
and the terrible slicing fall just before, as in
those nightmares that wake us, wet with shock.
Those who tyrannize quench for hours at a time,
and centuries, I'm sure, their dread of such
indifference. They make their subject abject,
stifle others to feel powerful themselves,
And for knowing that truth, you have had to leave
your native place. I wish music and I still could
soothe you, though I suspect this hombre and all his
shadows I wrestle with from Cambridge, this genius
did not enjoy the wonder of his apprehension ever.
He is, except in intelligence, so unlike you.
Your hands in repose still move me, your hands

in motion. And so, I would have you know
the way it stands for me toward you at this
juncture. As all governance is based,
if it is to be generous, on how a parent
feels toward a wanted child, I begin and end
with that. I would say yes to almost any
clear request from you, and sometimes yes, but
wait, and almost never no. Delay is no
in the diplomacy of caring. And when not asked,
since you have turned, it seems, from me, I
cannot force your will against our common pledge

to liberty in domestic polity as well as that
beyond home gates. I wish you had walked with me
this morning. As you did not, I write these
lines in fear of a solitude more unbearable
than any I have known.

To Newton: Of Italy, Nuns, and the Color Green

i
Nuns marry God, shun men, live cloistered
with women, or much alone in ways I've tried.
Green tomatoes in vinegar at midnight
was what the winged sisters fed us
in *clausura* in the convent in Urbino.
We came late,
missed the usual silent supper,
the other traveling students long asleep,
their *seicento lire* paid.
A dollar, or sometimes two, a night,
is what it cost in those days
to stay in Italian hostelries
and prayer, perhaps, but not required.

Time was the rule, closely observed.
Doors shut at eight at night, or ten at best.
We came late into Urbino,
the bus delayed in the old alluvial hills that roll
like tide-marked sand from Siena
where we had been to see the men in medieval costume
race the Palio on frantic horses
galloping in the cobbled, sloped piazza.

We found the cool church where green Duccio's old faces
stared from the madonna's arms like infants
who did not want to live. The green skin, mottled,
transparent as the green tomatoes from the later convent
garden, is, in paint, according to the guides,
an effect of time and light,
not the painter's constitution or intent.

We felt that green, spoke of it and laughed
at how aptly the color followed us onto the bus
that belched and spurted up and down the celebrated,
winding, ancient road between the hilltowns
and olive groves.
Half the passengers followed the vehicular example,
heads stuck out windows like exaggerated gargoyles
vomiting, resembling, in repose, Duccio's green infants,

until the old engine died, and we sat hours
in the country waiting for a replacement.

ii
Urbino was moonless, quiet, horseless, empty when we got there,
like a piece of purple velvet uncut in a shop, an iron grate
across the convent door we banged and banged on,
seeing the small sign CLAUSURA, meaning closed
as they made themselves, meaning vows of silence
variously practiced.

Elena composed a hasty note and passed the words
protezione delle giovani through the bars.
Shadows, faces, furtive whispering in the dark
and eyes that seemed to seek the highest section of the grate,
or God, and we were then told NO,
we could not sleep there now.

So much for the protection of young women.
My friend looked pale as birches in a summer storm,
shocked and about to snap. Another hat appeared,
white wings, sweet smile, the word *Botticelli*
and the door unlatched, spread just wide enough,
creaking, to let us through.

Elena looked like Primavera, hair that honeyed
and that long, eyes green as peridots, skin fair
and toffee-dappled. Everywhere through Italy
that summer, six weeks traveling as strangers,
we saw heads turn, hands reaching to feel
the hair and face. The Italians touch: the women
hair, cloth, anything to hand that is not flesh,
which is the men's domain. Did Galileo work then
with what's tangible as Newton did with what
cannot be seen?

iii
My friend of the snow statues, hockey fields,
and lost men, her father and her brother dead
the same year had put up a note on the wise kiosk
and hall: "Deserting a friend to get married.
Traveling in Italy and Germany July and August '61?"

Elena came to me like that, to guide me
with her knowledge and her book through her country,
to try to be without her mother in her favorite places,
to grow to independence having known it all her life.

She left me at the halfway point for her mother's arms
and home. And did not think it failure to love that way,
that much. Permitted attachment stunned me to tears.
That summer I came to Europe forbidden by my fiancé
to be with him in California. I should have understood.
I saw Elena and her mother liked each other,
chattered on and on and laughed and touched and, when
necessary, wept at pain and got over it. Or they were sick
and did not think of death but only *fegato* and camomile—
a small crisis of the liver, a call to the doctor,
penicillin maybe, herbal infusion always, *la cena*,
lunch, dinner, white tablecloths in restaurants and chianti
in house carafes, in good health or not, alone or with friends.

iv
The cubicles we slept in were separate, white and narrow
as tablecloths, linen draped over plaster and wood partitions,
a cross above the cot, thin mattress, blue-striped ticking
on the pillows stuffed with horsehair, white-starched pillowcase
and sheets bleached clean as vestments, the white of sunny countries,
and a wooden chair and table, lamp, cane seat, nothing more.
This could have been Orvieto or Ravenna. It could have been earlier
than midnight, the bus broken on a different bit of the journey.
I am remembering twenty-three years back, no journal kept.

I know those religious women wakened, as for a desperate
infant, did not ask us if we needed food, know
the oil on those green tomatoes they gave us at that hour
held the sun of the white bleached cloths. The women
scanned our faces once the Superior let us in, searched
as all mute people read with eyes, knew our hunger and
brought us to the long refectory table and fed us
bread and salad in candlelight.

The tiles of the communal bathroom were very white.
I spent half the night vomiting, thinking of vegetables,
how much we cast away of things that grow, as I cast

much away, thinking of husks of corn, the soft blond
tassels, spines of artichokes, giving it all up and wishing
I could find a use for everything, as often, I still wish.
I still like economy, and the uselessness of profusion
and birds dancing. The way those nuns sailed through
corridors with wide white cloth tiaras balanced them
and made them know the space around them, made them walk
as clearly as I always meant to write.

v
Those unwieldly costumes have their reason, as once
I saw a porcelain frog for sale by chance at the side of a road
the month my friend was moving from the home of her hurt marriage
to another house.

That year the rhododendrons clustered deep magenta, heavy
as some fruit. She had planted them as infant bushes, seen
how they became dark green, a fortress wall. And ached to leave
    them
even while she played badminton in their shade that last season
with her son. Knowing her new yard was smaller, less, in all ways
but acceptance, less, wanting an icon for all of us, of happenstance
and the shy joke that will arise more mischievous than desire,
and gentler, I saw that green, warty, shining, ceramic frog,
red tongue bulging, eyes like bulbs above puffed cheeks, was just
the thing for underneath a birdbath, or to put, half-hidden,
in a patch of shaded, half-wild, hiding violets.

I had to leave that job, an hour from home, on a road I never get to
anymore, or near. I never priced the bauble or bought the totem
of our hope in this unnatural condition: forced to hasty work,
shipwrecked, funds and attachment lost, jobs lean, when what we
    like
is thoroughness of time and care.

vi
Liking thoroughness of time and care, in deep night, emptied,
from the bathroom of white tiles I crept to the nun's white cubicle
in need of being held
and tried to understand
those who live and choose

a not-touching Godly comfort, all those fiancés
and later husbands who did not want us near them, wanted others,
less, more, men, Newton, whom I had read and written from that
    year in school.

Newton, did you ever wrestle in the night like this,
trying not to be alone for the rest of your life,
trying not to exploit, even in your thoughts,
particularly not there, given who you were,
how high the thoughts, someone you loved
and never shared the pleasure with? Did you love?
Do any of you think of how we think and feel?

The drapes of the cubicle were folded curves on curves.
I reached for God, my fingers finding cloth.
It turned to paper, soft as ash between nothing,
my own fingers. Which would not, there, on that thin,
holy mattress serve. Even he who loved matter so
turned to the mattress in the dark, I guess, or trust.

My arms reached around myself. I almost groaned.
And almost slept, and understood how Nora Joyce,
James Joyce's wife, understood he could not write
in middle age when near her, and felt like this
some nights, both of them, no doubt, but he could not
sleep unless she, who was no writer, wrote to him
of sex, in her words, he could read in a white room
an hour like this to keep the union whole and clean.
inviolate, together, as John Donne's separated
pointed compasses, aligned, even when alone.

With such passion at the knotting, knitting nuptials,
the rest followed, passionate devotion. Such consideration
and exchange, talk and fear, pain and answer: that was
marriage, not to God, I thought. And think I cried a little.
And know I slept.

Emilie du Châtelet to Elizabeth I of England
and to the Coming Age:
Of Nuns and Moons, Voltaire and Learned Women

i
I am frequently impatient at your notelessness.
When all those petty sonneteers had so many
silly words to leave behind. They called you

Cynthia, and meant the moon, pure and flat,
not rounded by the eye that, being round,
sees itself round in the moon or anything.

Your not-roundedness was half the trouble
with your reign, waxing and waning like
any woman, but failing to leave your print

on a prince. Some nights I have cast my voice
to that smile in the sky, to make sight
travel to the far side, make time a bellows

fanning with pressed air, fire opening
to breath. Such nights as these you also
must have tired of the past crowding

sleeplessness and tried to see the future
when a woman educated to our hilt and fashion
would not be a nun. I can see how you loved

your brother and hated the Regents who wanted
his throne, and strove, with Ascham's help,
to keep it from them. I know how you loved

your tutor, wanting, no doubt, to be a wife,
wanting ordinary touch, children, and for
a husband a man like Roger Ascham. Or Voltaire.

Isn't it strange how we adore the men
who teach us? Or not strange, given babyhood
when all first knowledge moves along the senses.

No wonder discovery carries passion in its curve
and boredom quenches it. And how you would have
had your age allied to James and married him

to rule together, how in the presence of any hope,
we know the truce of passion and affection
we call love. James was, after all, a scholar

like our tutors. He might have hoodwinked
your terror. Your father killing wives killed
your trust in husbands who were kings not given

to books and words of wisdom. But you left
the writing to the poets and scripture to your
successor, your father's child in that.

ii

Je suis frustrée que tu n'écris rien.
Or is it only lost, or given to the fire?
It is impolitic for monarchs to keep journals.

Alas. Though your virginity was hotly gloried
in and chided, publicly, the people were troubled
by your playful sport with men, and troubled too

with your not marrying. How is *it* for you,
they always want to know, the nameless little ones
who look at stars. How was it for you?

The same, I should think, as for anyone: too much
to bear alone. As it feels too much for anyone
to raise a child alone, as you half-raised Edward,

wanting him to be kind and king, no doubt,
not meaning to pamper him and have him die
at sixteen, querulous and sickly, not well loved.

The men who guarded him did not love him,
had not walked with him and dressed him, taught
him to arc his stream of gold into the porcelain

bowl at bedside, had not soaped him in the bath
and rubbed his babygums when he was pestered
with new teeth. O how we run our fingers over

wooden A's and rock the C with them and watch them
take the Y to suck to make curiosity become
hunger's companion. We owe our nurses and our tutors

everything but blood, those who keep us tended.
I pray for such a coming time when women
are as skilled as we who both knew this: unless some men

are in the early nursery and well gratified
by everyone for what that task requires
there is little hope of coupling without cutting

as your father did. He cuts me now, Voltaire.
And never wanted children, cuts me in my forty-fourth
year of life, as you were cut from dominion

in the forty-fourth year of reign. Too much.
They want us gone. And I am curious at the measure
of coincidence. Time has its periods like moons

and women. Babes suck as long as they are carried,
or twice as long. Shape follows time's pattern.
And number matters in ways I cannot guess.

And to the women in the coming gravity of time
which has its swells and seasons like the tides,
and to the men, we two stretch. Beyond the moon,

beyond the generation that has already found
how it is planted there, and what keeps it
from tumbling to our risen hurt and reaching.

The dumb show matters, how the parents play
together: I had that advantage. And some nights
would infuse it in your memory, give you a father

to match your generous mother in his delight.
Let's give you Ascham married to Anne Boleyn—
my parents were like that. And so they gave me

110

tutors, taught me Latin, as if I had been a boy.
But did not teach the boys to care for babies.
How do that? Saint-Lambert claims he wants a child

with me. I am—since all this search for knowing
how things burn, our endless visits to the iron
foundry—I am experimental. And, Elizabeth,

I may be pregnant even now. This young poet
is like my Latin tutor. Whole days come back,
the walks when he would tell me why I had to learn

the routes and roots of things, how everything
moves and is anchored to the earth.

iii
Tonight I've spent so long with Newton's
English, I can hear your voice come back at me,
Elizabethan, witty, fierce. To wit:

"You ask me how was it for me. Very well then.
I rejoin I know not what worlds are contained
in your 'it.' For methinks we were speaking

most particular of He and She, whereof
you misconster to say, the coming together
makes a mere neuter out of both. For see,

when the instruments sound their harmonies
and the revelers step to it, the fife
does not lose distinction from the drum

but rather each sounds more like the solitary
voices it uses. And even the clouds in melting
do not lose thereby their nature, but ensure

the seas the watery seeds whereof more clouds
will gather mist to denseness, and then rise.
On the white promontory of our Devon coast,

the clams and oysters, twin shells of creatures
that grew in different colonies, have pressed
together now to make a beachhead for the greedy

tides, but only in their dead shells. The living
stuff of creatures does not kill variety
in nature. And so, methinks this *it* of yours

is peevish and beshews a wish not to know
the fullness of yourself, or else a wish
to keep all things the same and uniform

as cannon for the work of war. Anything
alive is like an unicorn, one of a kind
though classes are similar in comport

and composition. Had there been any men
who loved the word as much as the world—
see what a difference a little L makes

in how they edit, text, or rolling heads—
I would have married. For no such man kills
wives, as my father did behead them

like careless dandelions in boys' hands
in spring. And they must needs be dancers,
and know the beat and rhythm that binds

the hid harmonies of things, or else jesters
who make us laugh together. O have you ever
heard two laughs alike? James should have

been born earlier to rule with me, or else
I later. I have seen him take my throne
for a moment and return it, seen him try it

on like a child a parent's cloak, wrapping
smallness to extinction, and smiling on surrender.
We have played that game for practice,

and in his carefulness of my sovereignty
I gave him his and would have governed
in delight with him for life."

iv
Newton, you are with me tonight, and all your
countrymen and forebears. I reach to the seeds

in the sky, time ahead and back, that fugue
you played with the Testaments.

Did you ever think of Martha in the scullery,
cleaning vegetables while her sister talked
philosophy with the Savior? Martha, the silent one,
her hands at work mashing a sweet cake with raisins,

carrots, apples, oats cooked soft for service
to the talkative guest, spiced with cinnamon
that lifted her to breathe slower and feel the way
the apples of her pointed against her robe,

the small carrot reached earthward. My body
changes with this late pregnancy. What do you
say to that, the moving shape of things, fixity
lost, the way the secret glaze will answer
the light of hope and passion in the eye?

To Newton: Of Freedom, the Plague, and the Unified Field

i
In 1665 when plague closed Cambridge down,
you went home to Woolsthorpe, and wrote
equations on the wall, and thought, at twenty-three,
about the earth and how you wanted it to shrink
to a small point, and could not for the life of you
find that year the calculus you needed to prove
such summing fair, so could not prove your theories
about gravity. And turned to light. In the plague year
Defoe later chronicled, you held the green glass
prism in your hand and thought of mass and distances.
Blind Milton wrote; you thought, and begged for God.

You had to wait another interval like that, some
twenty-two years more, to work the calculus
to correspond with what you knew was true.
And did not think of how the sound waves of the humming
planets plummet deep, and might be the whirr of time
itself, might talk to the particles at the center
of the things you saw, and shake them up.
You didn't ask, as philosophers this century have tried,
if possibly we are less free than we might think we like,
or like to be less free than in fact we are.
Gravity pins us to this earth, and lets us go
if we are clever enough to find the way around her pull.
As instinct calls us to overpopulate unless we sheathe
the arrows, catch the scattered seeds like stars in a wide net.

Imagine this of freedom, a parable:

A country where life enslaves whoever lives. Say
a weaving people who sleep in hammocks.
One night a peasant woman dreams she could be free.
She has six kids, picks jute all day in a torment of sun,
pounds stones for food.

Bring to her, sleeping still, a master of an alien religion
who has to tap her shoulder like any annunciatory angel
and asks her, do you want your freedom now? *Yes*, she says.
Of course. The angel laughs, and takes away the hammock
that holds the peasant, dreaming: notice, like the moment

before coming, before the rain breaks, sail fills, pick your
instance of that split instant of suspension, there is a stillness
before the peasant falls, before we all fall, to the waiting earth.

All my life I have wanted the hammock, the stars,
its points of contact holding threads that bind all things
to dancing with each other. In such a field of unison
the chorus sings of the small particles, their signature
like music, the charge of the electron, how it darts and
echoes with the sunspot cycle of the sun, the ton, the ton
of helium a second heaved toward us for light, for light,
and life. The sun is worth its weight of salt, dear Newton.

Our music plumbs the crystal of our being. Our octaves match
the seas, take mystery and make it home.
Our symphonies climb and echo in a sky so filled with burning
so far from us, here, wanting to feel close,
we could die if we did not reach for voice and instrument
to call to what we'll never altogether reach or know.

ii

The moment of entering the
  revolving door is like the
    moment of entering the turn-
      ing double ropes, the children
        are playing Double Dutch, as it
          is written, they are leading the
            way, chanting the helix and winding
            generosity easy as a skate-key
          tossed into the ascending and de-
        scending steps of the hopscotch
      grid. Their legs and arms extend
    into the day, making their bodies
  whole, and new again, making
them the shapes of chromosomes
    in play. They are present at
      the beginning, aleph in the
        first word, first world,
          letter of the joining code,
            its telling shape. I toss
          the two ropes for the children.
        I know we have been carrying
      these patterns from the start,
    turning wheels with our hands,
  turning ropes and clay, stitching
and knitting the shape of things
over and over. We jump, counting
  higher, we reach for the moon,
    double, we complete the moment
      of entering again and again.
        The needle enters cloth like this,
          embroidering, fastening as,
        at least once, the beloved enters
      and the whole body moves
    into the turning ropes.

iii
In a white, nubby bedspread, worn chenille,
I romped down the grass aisle on my father's arm
toward the yellow tents, the braided loaves.

This dress rehearsal holds my aunt's bedroom,
her double bed I've cribbed the cover from,
all the family fights and affection, my uncle,

who sleeps with her here, his early death lurking,
his horses and girlfriends well-loved. This is altruism,
this bedcover of the aunt and uncle training me

to walk clear, not trip, laugh at the rough, be ready
when I wear the antique veil the maid-of-honor will lift,
thin and light as onionskin, in a little while.

Something really terrible pinches my mother's face.
A secret she has kept from me. Cancer and she knows its
fierce extent. Surgery the next day for her, and she will

push me away when I return from journeying, push me
from her gaping chest, as if in losing me she lost
the giving breast. But today I see her unnamed pain,

and am light-hearted. I pretend it is only the arrangements
causing her tragic mask, the odor of fish filling the air
and no way to hide it. My father is so glad to give me

to another man. And I am happy in this easy cotton shift,
holding my father's arm, giddy, we are laughing
and it seems I am making him happy by this leaving

and completion. Later I understand he was thinking
he would get his wife back after the operation.
I am ready, past doubt in the formal garden, near

the assaultive turquoise of the pool. *I love you
with all my body* is what the old vow said,
is what I feel in the sunlight, the quartet practicing

Mozart to glide us, if we let the rhythm
instruct our approach to the canopy of marriage.
Do you love me with all your body?

On evidence, unlikely. Newton, it could have been you.
The color of chrome looms overhead.
A child is wailing for home.

iv
And I am alive despite this. Thinking of Hannah
and all the barren women crying to their God for children,
thinking of Hannah Newton.
>   I want to play
>   be a good sport,
>   an oddball of nature,
>   stick my neck out, poke the ball
>   in the goal, sink one, land one
>   let the fine net catch
>   my offering, the one seed entering,
>   hit a home run, score.
I am open as the net, the ark with all the animals,
the ark of the covenant, ready as a hammock
to embrace the guests, with arms and double scrolls.
Again and again.
>   Let the dance begin,
>   the contained explosion
>   popcorn blooming roses
>   light as warm snow in the pan,
>   from the first hard kernels
>   a small sun. O, even ice fills
>   a larger cup of air than the spill
>   of water. The smallest sip slips
>   into my waiting throat and I am alive
>   and kick my heels at the stars.

v
Newton, I think I understand, no, feel, I think I feel
the way you put yourself to task to keep from flying
into separate bits, as water flew from the flywheel

in your mother's garden. You found what you were
looking for, I want to say, by playing the percentages
and winning, and careful work. And coming before Darwin

and fearing the soft pull of creatures and their place in time
and accident, did not think to say selection is haphazard,
favoring chance, and partly made to order without constraint.

You lived long, although you neglected meals and followed God
more than rigid order. You lived to eighty-five and are
immortal, as such things go, avoided daydreams and wild

guesses. I have been more reckless, more in need of children
and of touch. Like your mother, any woman worth her
weight. I think often of your mother. Of Lucy, the mother

of us all, Australopithecus, how far we've come, how she
weighed in as if in chromosomal unison and rote answer at
fifty pounds, much smaller than the man, her mate. We

evolve by finding keys and entering more spacious rooms. We
start by copying, and then can use whatever comes to hand,
and vary it. She is full of infinite variety, this life of ours,

but there are ribbons, Love, dips and swells and shelves, we
don't store our provisions without intervals. Scallop shells are
ridged. We place our notes on staves. And all our looking at the
careful, beating gong of unity is to learn again and yet again
how to free the slaves.

vi
        I held a baby dandling on my knees
        at the valley of the afternoon.
        And she was tight and anxious till she leapt

        and bobbed and paid attention to my smiles.
        Her smile grew wings. She laughed.
        Her legs and shoulders loosened when

        she found the wooden bead around my neck
        and put it in her urgent mouth.

vii
O in anxiety and elation, in times of famine and of plenty
how we stoke the fire and mouth with food and wine

and smoke, and how the bliss, oh, the bliss of coming
through those gates, oh, the sweet victory, remembers

the ease and urgency of early feeding. O, how we once
made armies like the swimming hordes of sperm

to bomb the eye of cities, we can stop it if we see: how we
target to find security, sink the ball in the hole,

in the goal, the net, how the tennis court squares
our first shapes, and we ace the cornered cells

attempting over and over that first entry of sperm
to ovum, past barriers and all the mounting diapason

of growth and birth. O, yes, how we quest for the grail
and virtue and worth, search for the nameless unfound

pole, true North.

viii
Dearest, you knew and prove: where statement is question,
science is prayer. Thirty-one you framed, almost kin to
the Articles of Faith, to Light. You begged all that year
and this from such dense pages, that we not split hairs,

atoms, flesh and selves in brokenness, that the planet keep
intact in that solidity you saw as spacious before energy
was known to fly to mass, before X-ray, and laser beams
of sight and hurt and cure, before the unleashed hydrogen
and holocaust, you wrote, when light was only a warm
bath soaking into prisms at the close of a long day
without anyone to hold you close.

Your aether is embrace, the arms of affection that absorb
the small vibrations of the muscles, overwrought, wailing
the combat of trying to enter with questions the dark
stones, the cuticle of isolation that surrounds
even the clouds of atoms we now can see with heavy walls.

You would have wanted, then, to know, what aether is,
this ringing of coincidence that says, we match, we fit,

and go to wavelengths to keep things batched. Quantum
gravity could be a filing system not a fate,
something we might newly celebrate.
O Newton, I danced a whirling dance with you and tried
to push the thought of Plato's egg away; the lost half
he posited is with me now, and like the spiral crystal
at my center, I spin, I spin with you, alert to something
calling, coded, a Virginia reel: the healing chords

that twang our smallest strings, the focus and immensity
of getting lost in an activity like this, the entry of an actor
in a role and how that scrolls all past experience behind
the spoken words and fills the world with meaning.
The addict's needle and the drug of finding the right word
could have a common source: the chase for the vein of life
that makes us generous as genes who drown and go on
swimming to dry land and green.

ix
Here's Saint Francis on the golf course:
The course of things here is measured, stately.
Iron-cast, the clubs, if they could speak, would say.
When I see the players arc the dimpled seeds of play so far,
I half believe our sport names out all nine planets known,
the nine months of our first seas, cupped life, eons ago,
the first eyes and ions coming together in the heat.

It isn't only how the creatures speak to the ear,
but the simple shape of things, the tended grass, the way
the greens resemble the small things of the floating sea,
the cells of anything alive. The turtles in the damp spring
woods lay eggs like these white balls. Children toss the wild
ones to wet disaster. Haven't I done that? These, dry, travel
farther. Like comets. That much power in the drive.

Might putting greens be used to stop the slaughter, Father?

The cell, its smooth dark center enlarged and not flat,
a cup, drops of milk fountaining seed in the hole
and cheers for rising, scores, a birdie, the crowd soars, roars
delight and everything changes in due course.

We must keep a sandtrap in this formal garden, an uncut
meadow for the bees to dip in long stems
of lavender and goldenrod, wild places like prayer,
on a landscape of veils holding eggs numbered like stars
the fish pull through the deep ocean like reflections of
the Milky Way.

If golf could take us to the gulf-tides where amoebae
green the water and currents carry travelers in casual
gentleness along the warm, eyelit stream, might we be
surprised to peacefulness then? The fine grass at the center
pocks at the impact of a drive, my friend bends to the packed
earth, inserts a tee and lifts. "To let the roots breathe,"
she tells me. Our eyes meet. How do we write that care in

the game code, Love? It's all I really want to know of God.

x
My sons bring me to the Spectrum
to watch Yannick Noah play McEnroe,
tennis serving as a messenger of Love,
fifteen, thirty, forty, game. The camera
from the TV station overhead is labeled PRISM,
and my guides are glad to point out
the amiable connection.
They want Noah to win, Yannick, with his arcing body
break-dancing on the court, the way he falls and leaps
and pops with his racket in his hand. Look. His name
harps on the first great promise: there will be no other flood
that saves only the one containing vessel,
tiny crystal of paired molecules. Or is that enough?

From that first, massive, nuclear unfolding we are
in the recovery room all our lives
and seek to see writ large
when we are pressed
our own prehistory made bold
in shapely ways and joy
lest we ring ourselves around
with a halo of explosive missiles
imitate the sperm around the egg
make war in the sky in blinding radiance
and ignorance of why

122

this pattern makes us
mistakenly
feel safe.

Rape artists have lurked in the alleys of this ivy town.
But light is never known to follow crooked passages
nor to bend in the shadow. If theory could save
lives, language and biology have shown the way we play out
in our talk and all our war and sport,
in all our building and reports of upper limits, our scenes
of paradise and sacrifice, our processions to whatever altar,
the choreography of conception.

xi
Language deconstructs because first it falls together.
　　　　Root is the word, like *route*:
　　　　both traveling to anchor us,
　　　　come together from God knows where
　　　　in the world, from opposite stock
　　　　and source to marry as some lovers join
　　　　in identity, the odds against.

　　　　War is the word, like *whore*
　　　　joining spendthrift flesh, loss,
　　　　the camaraderie of the trenches.
　　　　O find, find another fellow
　　　　for your furrow, and all the earth
　　　　rumbles, turns, explodes.

　　　　Pray is the word, like *prey*:
　　　　moving to the center of what's lost,
　　　　the original act committing half
　　　　our splitting chromosomes to drown,
　　　　committing all but one nuclear missile
　　　　to genocide and unwitting holocaust.

　　　　Mass is the word, like *Messe*:
　　　　celebration of the body and the food,
　　　　eating, O yes, confusing
　　　　our messy masses in this feast,
　　　　this consummate love, twin beast of
　　　　sex we brood and brewed.

Won is the word, like *one*:
God, spiral frame of covenant and
commonwealth and wheel, bond
between matter and its other form
that spirits energy in twinkling
strings faster than losers feel left out.

In Latin, city walls fortified for defense,
like the boundaries of our very cells,
are the same sound and root as the word for
giving, ammunition and munificence bound
at the very core, like sperm and egg that mate.
The Greek horse sacked Ilium and all the spoils
of war followed penetration of that gift,
so much spilled, so much waste.

xii
These are the ruins of war.
The peaceful arts go nearly unrecorded.
Mother, I have been remembering your gifts,
the way you wrapped the haphazard packages
with paper bags, twine-tied the lopsided shapes,
whatever tissue you had on hand used for stuffing
around amorphous cookies wrapped in foil.

How the Cornish hens arrived once with a cousin
passing through Poughkeepsie, and we consumed them
in wonder at their small bones and savor,
trying to discover what spice, precisely,
released our appetites at midnight in the college dorm.

When I come home with presents from the Farmers'
Market, hand-crocheted elephants and plastic blocks
to give to babies still, miraculously, being born,
when I am without boxes to hold such gifts,
I hold the glazed and printed paper close around
the natural shapes, tie ribbon around food and jars,
the ribbed scrolls you showed me how to curl
by grazing along a blade. Carrying this latest
stuffed clown to the newest child born, I think

of being twenty again, laughing on the third floor
of Strong, waiting for Frannie, your namesake,

124

to come home from a date, Saturday night
at one o'clock in the morning. I contemplate
another small asteroid teetering on the dresser.
I wait to peel the covers from your latest bundle,
wait to pull out calendars and apricots and cashews
from the bottom of the bag. It is misshapen
as a sport of nature, a freak at a sideshow

of a small-town circus, the two-headed calf
preserved in the Cider and Donut Shop we ride to
on our antiquated bikes through the perfumed
orchards of Dutchess County. These shapes were
your sculptures, mother. With their offering,
you made us love oddity, taught us not to stone
the deviant, amazing as a waterfall, anything
that makes us breathless, this package of us
holding too much to bear alone.

The peaceful arts go nearly unrecorded.
In Sweden, I think, a Viking
man carved a plinth and steeped lasting color in the rock:
two snake-like figures and a rune in red.
The message to be seen in the Ashmolean
reads more or less, we think: *Here I, an aggrieved son,*
honor my father, dead.
Did you get to that other place, Newton, Oxford,
founded by a woman who ran from a man
who would have married her? She blinded him
and cured him so she could serve her God,
live chaste, and found the orders that became
the university for the monks. Frideswyde
her name, or so the story goes—
her work as pale and little noticed
as the message of her confrère
is vivid in stone.

The peaceful arts go so unrecorded.
There is a commonplace of British wild,
shown me by a man whose star-loving child
you might have known,
a man who, in his garden, keeps a wedge-shaped patch
unmowed so bees and hummingbirds and even snakes
may come to hide and sip the meadow flowers

125

and tall grasses left to grow and draw
the insects from the tended lawn.
The generations there come to toss the ball and watch the whirring
birds and play, the father's sons and daughters and their sons
and daughters laughing and unpestered and unbitten
even in the sweetness of their youth, its saving, coursing blood,
especially then.

To Newton: Argument and Recapitulation

What's a mere three hundred years
to lovers: that's the question.
Whether it's possible to meet
and mate in this space where I write, whether you,
meeting William Blake, would have changed the world
to peacefulness, whether he would have come to love you
as I do, though decently, without the sexual ache.
I being woman, loving, come eventually to that,
come to want the press and friction and caress
with a man I can't avoid. Blake knew your desperation.
Mine matches it. The hillside behind you, how it shapes
your back, how you do seem to ignore color itself,
color you studied so devotedly, a glass held in your hand.
Light was your friend. How the week of seven days
matches the rainbow: did that give you comfort?

Tracking the forest of the night to see light bend,
your father and your mother gone,
you watered heaven with dry tears,
avoided the spears of stars and turned to closer bodies:
planets, us, the tiger-colored heat of the blazing sun.
I want to comfort you as if you could come to bed.
That's the joke I laugh at. And if it were possible
I might not so have entered what you think and would
have made no effort to guess what you would make of
randomness, of quarks, all the indeterminacy we
put up with. There are tigers in this town I live in,
Einstein's second home, mascots of the university;
they stand, as we do, being some of us, on two legs and
shake paws, and dance and joke and laugh at gravity
and loss. I'd like to take the teeth out of war like that.
Get the missiles elsewhere, plan, millions of years
from now, to replenish the sun, impregnate the egg of
her with hydrogen. They don't belong here, those
unsheathed warheads like sperm let loose, jism, spawn.

And if I without your love and acting as if we could,
you understand, get together, make love, if in my mind,
trying as women do, without any prism, to understand
their lovers, I saw the electrons dance, saw a year as 365
degrees, a little bit too much to be a circle so lifting

to a spiral to go on, O yes, to rise in the sky matching the
crystal that we are, if I saw your name as clue, the
tonny weight of this globe married to time,
if I saw a world where science is held as God
and theory as theology and stumbled half by accident
to keep my hands to the page, and not where they would
wander, needing you, stumbled, I say, on Plato's
harmony of the spheres and thought I understood
his music might be newly true in ways he did not
conceive, what then?

Blake drew your desperation. Mine matches it.
And if, desperate, I dreamed, put poetry with science
and called it a unified field, even as I peeled away,
in this dream, the skin of narrow discipline,
wouldn't it be sad, and—picture a banana—laughable,
if, shut off from a man like you, more or less, who left,
I tumbled in the arms of an imagined sign of God?

Here's the argument again.
It keeps being you I wake to.
It's time to know.
To keep war from happening.
To save the earth and all the life we can.
What's a mere three hundred years to lovers?

It keeps being you I wake to, mornings, as if you were
conducting, your name on the radio, after a symphony playing
in the clouds of waking up, rising like the smoke of some
vanished, burning dream. I can see the way you have brought
all the instruments together, like coins, a hillside
of gold sovereigns. I can feel you at a door, about to lead,
suddenly grown human, wondering what is on the other side.

All music falls like that,
into openings, half-knowing, as love moves
accidentally with purpose, among familiars.
Laughter on entering, laughter
at the way a plant pokes the air, green leaves, jagged edges
against a curtain. Tongue-tied, thick with dream this gray
dawn, I can see you understand we want to make the sea more
alive, the weave thicker, with some pale grass
even the lithest antelopes have yearned not to crush.

Emilie du Châtelet Sees into the Future:
Her Infant beside Her the Day Before She Dies

This late birth and all the lying in makes me restless.
As childhood naps I did not want to take.
That one percent chance, or less
of not being here at the end of deep sleep,
the knowing, before knowledge,
what a percent is,
the answer, before number, of prayer.

Let me wake or take me safely.
Let me not be taken,
the child asks the dark.

Waking astonished, I bring her to the day,
as if in listening to her
speak like that, to such a God,

I would be placated in the rage I feel,
or would, at having to leave now.
The air gives clear purple at the side

of the house, flowers I have never seen before,
visions of the fever, maybe. I must get out
to gather color. Cannot. This solitude

is like desire that can no longer be waived.
O, I have seen the empty branches.
I have missed the martins and swallows,

imagined them keeping away, as I,
my heart unable to sustain the opening
like that darkness where the birds peck,

do not come back, do not.

To Newton: Of Good Measure and the Dark

For good measure, we say
a thing twice, two different
ways, in case it isn't picked up

the first time, as at home
we always added an extra
tablespoon of honey to the batter

and another to the dewy icing
we drizzled over the finished cake.
We took an extra apple,

a dozen spare paper napkins
on the picnic that meant
room for spills, for one more,

the possibility of the shipwrecked
crashing our party, this shore.
We set repetition against

disaster and simple cussedness.
For good measure, we said, until
I knew its opposite. Consider

cutting cloth with bad measure,
a ruler cut short like a king
dead at seventeen, the hot water

run out before the soap is off,
the shower cold. This is surely
why we want a baker's dozen

in all things, thirteen eggs to hedge
against breakage, a long ton,
a child's hug before sleep,

that measure of time asked
of a parent, the warm embrace
loosening comfort like a honey

glaze. Good measure takes me
past the careful balance of
raising children, lets the coastline

grow, that long probe of light
scores every ridge and wrinkle,
winks away resistance, maps

and marks me before
the terrifying and im-
measurable dark.

To Newton: Of Wild Geese and King Lear

Winter's not yet gone,
when the wild geese fly that way,
and today, reading,
I am on that first linoleum,
building and tumbling alphabet blocks,
red letters, light blue rim.
I can feel the deep pleasure of all beginnings,
that sweet pressure of pleasure
among the geese at my grandmother's house,
the first stick I rode
and took from between my legs,
to chase their honking.
There is no chastity, Newton,
only finding the integral
that chooses the least unkindness.

There are mazes
more amazing than those we know
from the old stories.
Many paths lead to the center.
Pray the empty room is not sheathed in metal,
vaulted and locked with double keys that have been lost.
In such a fix, what hero
could beam what metal-shattering light of rescue, arrive
with that breathless discovery of being safe
and known and answered?

Just this week
my sons have left the house again,
grown children gone to their father,
that house where the cradle
they slept in as infants holds wild plants.
The leaves strain toward the light.
I come home to find silence,
the door to their two rooms shut,

and behind the doors
a second silence, yours.
I remember the cradle
with each of them in it, and the feel of desire,
the day each of them was conceived,

the wet leaves, the saying please, the answer,
that one time, yes.

And, given stories
of unusual couplings,
I see there is nothing remarkable
I have ever imagined,

only the bud in the candle,
the roughness of need and a beard
pressing like urgency
in the dusk. I remember the newness

of first things creeping,
can smell the blind nuzzle of cinnamon in the air,
the press of pen, and bodies.
I wanted the children to know me
remembering the feel of enough time,
the long afternoons of ducks and geese
behind my grandparents' house.
I wanted to know what they might remember,
before memory framed it with experience.
It was difference I liked, not sameness,
answer not the power of refusal,
play, not the stretch for ambition's hazard.
Now, I look for them
and signs of their life
in this room they sometimes live in,
the way I once looked for tricks of memory,
or someone like you,
to break free.

I can see the cradle,
the antique store I found it in,
and the carpenter, who sawed and glued
the mahogany slats and spindles. I thought
it might be a comfort
like a prism bending light,
the way the geese still fly
like the pointed stick
in the winter sky
of me.

Thinking of Newton, I Look into the Future

If I could take a prism and bend all love,
as glass fans an arm of light to a fingered rainbow,
if I could follow each color of love
into the think distraction at the broad end
where the spectrum meets plain air,
this morning, waking to red berries
on the tops of black-boned winter trees,
simple red dawn making memories of fruit
in orchards, red currants drooping from roadside
branches like lazy grapes that would not grow like
grapes, not so purple or so large—
this morning would represent the love of hope.

The hillside is white. Loyal, it keeps the tracks of skiers,
their twisting twin shadows, the history
of some blank helix, unwound, exploiting gravity.

I know again the release from friction ice
and slick surfaces accomplish. My children
do not come sledding in big snows anymore,
do not hoot in striped woolen hats and fringed scarves
on the carved slopes of the Chateau.
They ski in the local Alps, skiing as distinct from sledding
as purple light from green, godhead
from infancy. They stand on two moving legs.

And race through white air until what they cut
is solid as the silver water a diver slices through,
solid as iridescent muscles and ligaments of the slain.

Everyone is gone from home.

Let them come back.
Let them fall into the necessary posture of love,
this soft turtle of us lying down,
yearning between mantles of damp rock.
Let them lie close to the snow, rise
with the wheels and poles behind them,
spinning the code of abandon, the course of ongoing,

easy as the small pattern, early, unremembered,
behind them
in the downhill run
of sustenance.

To Newton as Daedalus

You tried to hold up your friend whom, earlier, you felt
you had betrayed. He fell again, confused and hopeless,
and you grieved while he was in hospital.

After such flying there is only dropping out,
as from the clear blue, dropping out of this green place
with its gray skies and the stone that holds

the light on sunless days. Buff stone, these buildings,
and the tall windows of the old Quaker chapel:
leaving this behind, with maps that point the way,

color-coded, you lose altitude and breath. Where does it come from,
the heart to say "I will push through, alone, forever,"
as if a child might emerge from the labor,

making bearable the bearing, burden, the struggle and the strain?
Push, yes, though there is nothing, pour, pant and do not cry out,
scream inwardly because they cannot see why

you might be hurting. There is God, yes, and the grass is green
in winter and even once limed, but only thinly, and, thank goodness,
our small vessels do not stiffen or explode

on climbing. My eyes read years and yours and we cannot do this
to each other forever. Or can we? Given where you are, where I am.
As I drive in this bright sun, the blackness of a crow's wing

cuts sight. It is again the darkness of not looking at you
as I tell you how deeply distinct our lives are, how you have
so much you belong to, holding you up in this darkness.

The universe is your community, the stars your friends
holding you up as wings held up those who moved like Daedalus,
like Zeus to Leda, to some great moment, or the sun.

To Newton from the Recovery Room

After all I am alive despite this.

Small changes can be monumental.

I ask my son if he believes
the whole history of each of us
might be imprinted in us everywhere,
all the implantations and loss
and branching shape. He is shocked
and laughs and thinks he knows
he could remember football games
and chromosomes and other times
he knew my hypotheses were only
pastimes lacking story. *Crazy lady,*
Mom, to think the players
and the ball add up to chromosomes
and your version of the fall.

I love him from all my body.

I love the whole body of them both,
this one flanging shoulders now,
pushing downy hairs, and bulges,
deepening the need and thought,
the voice and knowledge of his anger,
mine, and all the centuries of war.
He has learned to leave the house
and walk in the cold air instead of
lifting the stenciled chair
to score legmarks in linoleum.

His younger brother calls him bow.
And bough. His green eyes and easy
ambling grace take breath away from
the unprepared. We never speak of beauty
in a boy. Beautiful is hard.

When I was growing up
to be a boy meant it was
only easier

to pee in the woods or
from a rowboat

easier to fit into
tight jeans
the crooks of trees
except for some
flat-bellied
flat-buttocked girls.
To be a boy meant

it was always harder
to have a beautiful
*any*thing, like
eyes, handwriting,

way of slipping on
tip-toe between
the desks and chairs
giving out corrected

spelling tests. The ink
was blue-black and
indelible. I wanted
the first writing

with the fountain pen
my parents gave me
for my seventh birthday
to be as shapely

as Tommy's body
wise-eyed
the O's and A's
open and alive.

Small changes can be monumental.

The children are something apart, alive despite
the weather. Here, washing up in hazy weather, the two taps
blend in one spigot running harmonies of hot and cold.

Sometimes, washing up alone, I think I feel the separate strands
of braided water, as I see my hand gesture in my child's hand,
see in that same moment the father's raised eyebrow

in the son's face. Last Thanksgiving, doing dishes, the neckbones
of the turkey came undone in my hand, like a necklace
on a tired cord, jewels I had to keep for beauty, and evidence

of I don't know what. Tonight my dimmed sight moves to the shelf,
the turkey bones still delicate as mouse skulls there. I see
terriers in the spinal column, bloomed iris, doghead of dreams.

I am remembering the hero of stone and tooth and vision
who rode horseback in China and planted a jaw in a sterile
barrow in England to suck out fame for a friend, it seems.

On the edge of objectivity, given up for friendship, truth bent
for affection like an ordinary white lie, scientific sight—
its press for truth distorted by need, this hoax is part

of his repertoire who loved the universe and chided God
for some obscure proof of forgiveness, there, God knows,
always there. In the presence of bones, I touch

that betrayal in ways I cannot bear to know again.

     Small changes can be monumental.

     Tell me then where fancy lies?
     Simple, not fancy. Simple, and so elegant.
     How much the firstborn child insults
     a wanting parent's place,
     as circumcision is acknowledgment
     of the desire to murder
     jealousy itself
     the infant whose breath and blood and need
     have come between
     time and the joining place.

     As Newton took the planets'
     dance indoors and scratched it

on his walls in search of
the choreography inside,

we gather all the fragments
as we age, if we are lucky.
No proof of cumulation,
only summer summing seed

and rain and labor, only that
so many stars in coincidence
in the empty sky provoke
belief in light and space

charting some commerce
between the source
and us. I remember a pilot
flying solo in the wilderness

of night, the plane upturned,
the stars exchanged for earth,
memory believing heaven was down
there until a wind or shudder

of another engine in the starry
emptiness restored the world.

Small changes can be monumental.

Just last year at the dance concert,
the players, half naked,
breasts bare, wearing skis indoors
to root them on the wooden floor

fell and fell, arching their bodies,
forever, it seemed, on those flat
stilts, that raised them beyond
ordinary torsion, suspended

collapse, confirmed and held them
against tumbling. The double ties
that grounded those two couples
bound them to grace and patience

like religious vows, over and over,
known, taken, they turned
somersaults, their antlered feet
making points of contact

without combat. The extended feet
of one held her partner firm
and so more mobile. How did
the choreography symbolize those moves?

They press and release. They do not fight.

We are in the recovery room all our lives,
Newton. After you had gone to the other side,
gone to a sexless, easy exchange with colleagues,
the body become intelligence, the great, pubic
root-system and massive trunk
grown like a chestnut given to feeding,
the leaves spread in two portions,
like the brain itself, a parliament
of singing birds filled with light,
after I felt the full shock
of your denial forever,
I dreamed you reformed, came home,
needed need and the great pleasure
of touch and hunger, the great thirst
that makes its own fountains,
needed, I say, to use your body,
press, kiss, caress.
And so, awkward as a leggy grasshopper,
green and new as the spinning top
belonging to the boy you were that happiest
spring, you lay all knees and elbows
in my arms, grew warm, and we wept together
laughing before the full wetness of the dive,
the long slide to wordlessness
except for thank-yous at the fine completion,
astonishment at the end
before our bodies curled together
in this bed, before sleep
and waking alone. In the early light
I am a Mexican wedding hammock,

double, ample, *matrimoniale* of pure cotton,
white as the hair of my grandparents.
I hold the wedding couple
all night in my woven threads
like a sieve of exhaustion,
the borders of their lives.
I taste their joy.
I touch the arc of their regret.
I breathe the song of their sleep.